Financial Savvy for Entrepreneurs

Essential Tools and Strategies for Managing Business Finances

TONY TUCKER

© Copyright 2024 by TONY TUCKER
All Rights Reserved

The presentation of the information is without contract or any type of guarantee assurance. The trademarks that are used are without any consent, and the publication of the trademark is without permission or backing by the trademark owner. All trademarks and brands within this book are for clarifying purposes only and are the owned by the owners themselves, not affiliated with this document.

Table of Contents

Chapter 1

Introduction to Financial Management

Understanding Financial Literacy

Financial literacy is a crucial life skill that empowers individuals to make informed and effective decisions with their financial resources. It encompasses a variety of topics, including budgeting, saving, investing, and understanding credit. Developing financial literacy helps people navigate the complexities of the financial world, avoid common pitfalls, and achieve long-term financial stability.

Imagine a young professional, Emma, who has just started her first job. Excited about her newfound independence, she quickly realizes the importance of managing her finances wisely. Emma's journey toward financial literacy begins with understanding the basic principles of budgeting. Budgeting is the cornerstone of financial health, as it allows individuals to track their income and expenses, ensuring that they are living within their means. Emma learns to categorize her expenses into fixed costs like rent and utilities, and variable costs like groceries and entertainment. By doing so, she gains clarity on where her money is going and can identify areas where she can cut back if necessary.

Saving is another critical aspect of financial literacy. Emma decides to adopt the 50/30/20 rule, a popular budgeting method where 50% of her income goes toward necessities, 30% toward discretionary spending, and 20% toward savings. This framework helps her build an emergency fund, which is essential for covering unexpected expenses such as medical bills or car repairs. Financial experts recommend having three to six months' worth of living expenses saved in an easily accessible account. Emma's commitment to saving not only provides her with a safety net but also instills a sense of security and financial confidence.

Investing is a powerful tool for growing wealth over time, and it requires a solid understanding of different investment options and strategies. Emma learns about the importance of starting early, as the power of compound interest can significantly increase her wealth over the years. She explores various investment vehicles, including stocks, bonds, mutual funds, and real estate. Diversification is a key principle she adopts, spreading her investments across different asset classes to reduce risk. Emma also familiarizes herself with retirement accounts such as 401(k)s and IRAs, taking advantage of employer matching contributions to maximize her retirement savings.

Understanding credit is another vital component of financial literacy. Credit can be a double-edged sword; it can help individuals achieve their financial goals, but if not managed wisely, it can lead to significant debt and financial distress. Emma educates herself on how credit scores are calculated and the factors that influence them, such as payment history, credit utilization, and length of credit history. She learns the importance of paying her bills on time and keeping her credit card balances low to maintain a healthy credit score. Emma also understands the benefits and risks of using credit cards, choosing to use them responsibly to build her credit history without falling into the trap of high-interest debt.

Debt management is another crucial aspect of financial literacy. Emma realizes that not all debt is bad; for instance, student loans and mortgages can be considered good debt if they are used to invest in her education or home. However, she is wary of high-interest debt, such as credit card debt, which can quickly spiral out of control. Emma develops a strategy to pay off her debts systematically, prioritizing those with the highest interest rates. She also learns about debt consolidation and refinancing options that can help lower her interest rates and simplify her payments.

Financial planning and goal setting are essential for achieving long-term financial success. Emma sets short-term, medium-term, and long-term financial goals, such as paying off her student loans, saving for a vacation, and buying a house. She creates a detailed plan to achieve these goals, regularly reviewing and adjusting it as needed. Emma understands that financial planning is not a one-time activity but an ongoing process that requires discipline and foresight.

Insurance is another important topic within financial literacy. Emma learns about different types of insurance, such as health insurance, life insurance, and property insurance, and how they can protect her from significant financial losses. She evaluates her insurance needs based on her lifestyle and financial situation, ensuring that she is adequately covered without overpaying for unnecessary policies.

Taxes are an inevitable part of life, and understanding the basics of taxation is a crucial element of financial literacy. Emma educates herself on how income taxes work, the difference between gross and net income, and the importance of filing her taxes correctly and on time. She also learns about tax deductions and credits that can reduce her taxable income, such as those for education expenses and retirement contributions. By understanding the tax system, Emma can make informed decisions that minimize her tax liability and maximize her savings.

Financial literacy also involves being aware of consumer rights and protections. Emma learns about laws and regulations that protect consumers from fraud and unfair practices, such as the Fair Credit Reporting Act and the Truth in Lending Act. She understands her rights when it comes to disputing errors on her credit report, protecting her personal information, and avoiding scams. This knowledge empowers Emma to make informed decisions and seek recourse if she encounters any financial issues.

Finally, financial literacy encompasses the ability to navigate the ever-evolving financial landscape. With the rise of digital banking, online investing platforms, and financial technology (fintech) innovations, staying informed about new tools and trends is essential. Emma takes advantage of educational resources, such as financial blogs, podcasts, and online courses, to continuously improve her financial knowledge. She also seeks advice from financial professionals when needed, recognizing the value of expert guidance in making complex financial decisions.

Emma's journey toward financial literacy illustrates the transformative power of understanding and managing one's finances. By mastering the basics of budgeting, saving, investing, credit, debt management, financial planning, insurance, taxes, consumer rights, and staying informed about financial innovations, individuals can achieve financial stability and build a secure future. Financial literacy is not just about acquiring knowledge; it's about applying that knowledge to make sound financial decisions that align with one's goals and values. Emma's story serves as a reminder that anyone can become financially literate with dedication and the right resources, ultimately leading to a more prosperous and fulfilling life. In addition to the foundational elements of financial literacy, there are several advanced concepts and strategies that can further enhance one's financial well-being. Once Emma has a solid grasp of the basics, she begins to explore these more sophisticated aspects of personal finance.

Importance of Financial Management for Entrepreneurs

Entrepreneurship is an exhilarating journey that demands not only innovative ideas and relentless drive but also astute financial management. Financial management is the backbone of any successful business, enabling entrepreneurs to make informed decisions, allocate resources efficiently, and ensure long-term sustainability. Understanding its importance can spell the difference between a thriving enterprise and a struggling one.

Consider Sarah, a budding entrepreneur with a passion for sustainable fashion. She has a brilliant idea to create eco-friendly clothing, but without a solid grasp of financial management, her dream could falter. Her journey underscores the critical role of financial management in entrepreneurship.

From the outset, Sarah realizes that creating a detailed business plan is essential. This plan outlines her business goals, target market, competitive analysis, and financial projections. The financial projections, in particular, are crucial as they provide a roadmap for her business's financial future. These projections include income statements, cash flow statements, and balance sheets, which help her anticipate revenues, expenses, and profits.

Securing funding is often the first major financial hurdle for entrepreneurs. Sarah explores various financing options, including bootstrapping, loans, and seeking investors. Each option has its pros and cons. Bootstrapping allows her to retain full control of her company but may limit her growth potential due to limited funds. Loans provide immediate capital but come with the burden of repayment and interest. Investors offer substantial funding and valuable expertise but require giving up a portion of ownership. Understanding these options and choosing the right mix is a critical decision that impacts her business's trajectory.

Effective cash flow management is another cornerstone of financial management that Sarah must master. Cash flow, the movement of money in and out of the business, is the lifeblood of any enterprise. Sarah learns that even profitable businesses can fail if they run out of cash. She implements strategies to monitor and manage her cash flow, such as forecasting cash needs, maintaining a cash reserve, and invoicing promptly. By doing so, she ensures that her business has enough liquidity to cover day-to-day operations and unexpected expenses.

Budgeting is a fundamental aspect of financial management that helps entrepreneurs like Sarah control costs and plan for the future. She creates a detailed budget that outlines her expected income and expenses. This budget serves as a financial blueprint, guiding her spending decisions and helping her stay on track. Regularly reviewing and adjusting the budget allows her to respond to changes in the business environment and seize new opportunities.

Financial management also involves understanding and managing costs. Sarah categorizes her costs into fixed and variable expenses. Fixed costs, such as rent and salaries, remain constant regardless of her business's performance, while variable costs, such as materials and shipping, fluctuate with sales. By analyzing her cost structure, Sarah identifies areas where she can reduce expenses without compromising quality. For instance, she negotiates better terms with suppliers and explores more cost-effective marketing strategies.

Pricing strategy is another critical component of financial management. Setting the right price for her eco-friendly clothing involves balancing several factors, including production costs, competitor pricing, and perceived value. Sarah conducts market research to understand what her target customers are willing to pay and models different pricing scenarios to determine their impact on profitability. A well-thought-out pricing strategy helps her attract customers while ensuring that her business remains profitable.

As Sarah's business grows, she faces the challenge of managing working capital. Working capital, the difference between current assets and current liabilities, is essential for maintaining day-to-day operations. Sarah learns to manage her inventory levels to avoid tying up too much cash in unsold goods while ensuring she can meet customer demand. She also strengthens her relationships with suppliers and customers to negotiate favorable payment terms and improve her cash conversion cycle.

Debt management becomes increasingly important as Sarah's business expands. While taking on debt can fuel growth, it also introduces financial risk. Sarah carefully evaluates her business's ability to service debt and avoids overleveraging. She explores options such as refinancing to secure lower interest rates and consolidating debt to simplify repayment. By managing debt prudently, she maintains her business's financial health and flexibility.

Investment decisions are another critical aspect of financial management. Sarah evaluates potential investments in new products, technologies, and markets. She conducts thorough cost-benefit analyses to determine the expected return on investment and assesses the associated risks. Diversifying her investments helps mitigate risk and ensures that her business is not overly reliant on a single revenue stream.

Tax planning is an often-overlooked element of financial management that can significantly impact an entrepreneur's bottom line. Sarah works with a tax professional to understand her business's tax obligations and identify strategies to minimize her tax liability. This includes taking advantage of tax credits and deductions, planning for estimated tax payments, and structuring her business in a tax-efficient manner. By proactively managing her tax obligations, Sarah maximizes her after-tax income and reinvests savings back into her business.

Financial reporting and analysis provide valuable insights into the health of Sarah's business. She regularly reviews financial statements to monitor performance and identify trends. Key financial ratios, such as gross margin, return on assets, and current ratio, help her assess profitability, efficiency, and liquidity. By analyzing these metrics, Sarah makes data-driven decisions that drive her business forward.

Risk management is another essential aspect of financial management for entrepreneurs. Sarah identifies potential risks to her business, such as market fluctuations, supply chain disruptions, and regulatory changes. She develops a risk management plan that includes strategies for mitigating these risks, such as diversifying suppliers, securing insurance coverage, and staying informed about industry regulations. By proactively managing risks, Sarah protects her business from unexpected setbacks and ensures its long-term viability.

Finally, financial management involves planning for the future. Sarah sets both short-term and long-term financial goals for her business. These goals provide direction and motivation, helping her stay focused on what matters most. She creates a strategic financial plan that outlines the steps needed to achieve these goals, including expanding her product line, entering new markets, and increasing profitability. Regularly reviewing and updating this plan ensures that her business remains on a path of sustainable growth.

Sarah's journey as an entrepreneur illustrates the critical importance of financial management. By mastering these principles, she not only ensures the survival of her eco-friendly clothing business but also positions it for long-term success. Financial management is not just about numbers; it's about making informed decisions, managing resources effectively, and building a strong foundation for growth. Entrepreneurs who prioritize financial management are better equipped to navigate challenges, seize opportunities, and achieve their dreams. Sarah's dedication to financial management transforms her business from a fledgling startup into a robust enterprise. As she expands her business, she faces new financial challenges and opportunities, each requiring careful consideration and strategic planning. Her story highlights several additional aspects of financial management that entrepreneurs must navigate.

Key Financial Terms and Concepts

Understanding key financial terms and concepts is fundamental for anyone venturing into the world of business. Grasping these concepts not only demystifies the financial landscape but also empowers entrepreneurs to make sound decisions. Let's delve into some essential financial terms and concepts that every entrepreneur should know.

Revenue, often referred to as sales or turnover, is the total amount of money generated from selling goods or services. It's the top line of an income statement and represents the inflow of resources. For example, if Jane runs a bakery, her revenue includes all the money received from selling cakes, bread, and pastries. Revenue is crucial because it indicates the business's capacity to generate income from its core activities.

Expenses are the costs incurred to generate revenue. They can be categorized into fixed and variable expenses. Fixed expenses, such as rent and salaries, remain constant regardless of the business's performance. Variable expenses, like raw materials and shipping costs, fluctuate with production levels. Jane's bakery, for instance, has fixed costs for her shop's rent and variable costs for ingredients used in baking. Managing expenses effectively is vital for maintaining profitability.

Profit, or net income, is the amount of money left after subtracting all expenses from revenue. It's the bottom line of the income statement and indicates the business's financial health. Positive profit means the business is earning more than it spends, while a loss indicates the opposite. Jane calculates her profit by deducting her expenses from her revenue. Understanding profit helps entrepreneurs gauge their business's sustainability and success.

Gross profit is another important concept, representing the difference between revenue and the cost of goods sold (COGS). COGS includes direct costs attributable to the production of goods sold by the company. For Jane, this would be the cost of flour, sugar, and other ingredients. Gross profit helps in analyzing the efficiency of production and the pricing strategy.

Operating profit, also known as operating income, is derived from subtracting operating expenses from gross profit. Operating expenses include all costs associated with running the business, except for interest and taxes. This figure provides insight into the business's profitability from its core operations, excluding the effects of financial and tax decisions.

Cash flow represents the net amount of cash moving in and out of the business. Positive cash flow indicates that a company's liquid assets are increasing, enabling it to settle debts, reinvest in the business, pay expenses, and provide a buffer against future financial challenges. Jane monitors her cash flow to ensure she has enough cash to buy supplies and pay her staff. Understanding cash flow is crucial because even profitable businesses can fail if they run out of cash.

Assets are resources owned by the business that have economic value. They can be classified into current and non-current assets. Current assets, like cash and inventory, are expected to be converted into cash within a year. Non-current assets, such as property and equipment, are long-term investments. Jane's bakery assets include her ovens (non-current) and her inventory of flour and eggs (current). Knowing the value of assets helps in evaluating the business's financial strength.

Liabilities are obligations that the business must pay in the future. They can be current (due within a year) or long-term (due after a year). Current liabilities include accounts payable and short-term loans, while long-term liabilities might include mortgages or bonds. Jane's bakery might have current liabilities like bills for ingredients and long-term liabilities like a loan for her shop. Managing liabilities is essential for maintaining the business's financial stability.

Equity, also known as owner's equity or shareholders' equity, represents the owner's claim on the assets of the business after all liabilities have been deducted. It includes capital invested by the owner and retained earnings. For Jane, equity would be the money she initially invested in her bakery plus any profits she has reinvested in the business. Equity indicates the net value of the business and is crucial for assessing its financial health.

The balance sheet is a financial statement that provides a snapshot of a company's financial position at a specific point in time. It lists assets, liabilities, and equity, following the fundamental accounting equation: Assets = Liabilities + Equity. Jane's balance sheet shows her bakery's resources, obligations, and the residual interest of the owners. The balance sheet helps in assessing the company's financial stability and liquidity.

The income statement, also known as the profit and loss statement, summarizes revenues, expenses, and profits over a specific period. It provides a detailed account of how the net income (or loss) was achieved. Jane's income statement would detail her bakery's sales, the cost of ingredients, staff salaries, rent, and the resulting profit or loss. This statement is essential for understanding the business's profitability and operational efficiency.

The cash flow statement tracks the flow of cash in and out of the business over a specific period. It is divided into three sections: operating activities, investing activities, and financing activities. Jane uses her cash flow statement to monitor her bakery's liquidity and ensure she can meet her financial obligations. This statement is crucial for understanding the business's cash position and operational health.

Depreciation is the process of allocating the cost of tangible assets over their useful lives. It reflects the wear and tear of assets as they are used in the business. For example, Jane's ovens will depreciate over time as they are used in baking. Depreciation affects the value of assets on the balance sheet and the expenses on the income statement. Understanding depreciation helps in accurately representing the value of assets and the cost of using them.

Accounts receivable represent money owed to the business by customers for goods or services delivered but not yet paid for. Jane's accounts receivable would include outstanding invoices for large orders. Managing accounts receivable is crucial for maintaining healthy cash flow and ensuring timely collection of payments.

Accounts payable are amounts the business owes to suppliers for goods or services received but not yet paid for. Jane's accounts payable might include bills for flour and sugar purchased on credit. Managing accounts payable effectively ensures that the business maintains good relationships with suppliers and avoids late payment penalties.

Break-even analysis determines the sales volume at which total revenues equal total costs, resulting in neither profit nor loss. For Jane, it's crucial to know how many cakes she needs to sell to cover her fixed and variable costs. This analysis helps in setting sales targets and pricing strategies.

Liquidity ratios, such as the current ratio and quick ratio, measure the business's ability to meet short-term obligations. These ratios are vital for assessing the company's short-term financial health. Jane monitors her liquidity ratios to ensure her bakery can pay its bills on time.

Profitability ratios, such as the net profit margin and return on equity, assess the business's ability to generate profit relative to sales, assets, or equity. These ratios help in evaluating the overall financial performance and operational efficiency. Jane uses profitability ratios to gauge her bakery's success and identify areas for improvement.

Leverage ratios, such as the debt-to-equity ratio, measure the degree to which the business is financed by debt versus equity. These ratios indicate the financial risk associated with the business's capital structure. Jane evaluates her leverage ratios to ensure her bakery maintains a healthy balance between debt and equity.

Understanding these key financial terms and concepts provides a solid foundation for entrepreneurs. They form the language of business, enabling clear communication with investors, lenders, and other stakeholders. For Jane, mastering these concepts means she can effectively manage her bakery's finances, make informed decisions, and drive her business towards long-term success. Entrepreneurs who invest time in understanding these fundamentals are better equipped to navigate the financial landscape and achieve their business goals. One of the foundational principles in financial management is the concept of budgeting. A budget is a detailed financial plan that outlines expected revenues and expenses over a specific period, usually a year. For Jane, creating a budget for her bakery involves estimating her sales, costs of ingredients, labor expenses, rent, utilities, and other operating costs. By comparing her actual performance against the budget, Jane can identify variances, understand their causes, and make necessary adjustments. Budgeting helps in setting financial targets, planning for future growth, and ensuring the business remains on track financially.

Setting Financial Goals

Setting financial goals is a critical step for any entrepreneur aiming to navigate the complex world of business and achieve long-term success. Financial goals serve as a roadmap, guiding business decisions and strategies, and ensuring that the enterprise remains focused and aligned with its overall mission. They provide measurable milestones that help track progress, motivate the team, and facilitate adjustments when necessary. By setting clear, achievable financial goals, entrepreneurs can better manage resources, anticipate challenges, and seize opportunities.

The first step in setting financial goals is to define the vision and mission of the business. These foundational elements provide context and direction for the financial goals. The vision is the long-term aspiration of the business, while the mission outlines the purpose and primary objectives. For example, if Jane's bakery's vision is to become the leading provider of organic baked goods in her city, her financial goals will be tailored to support this vision, such as increasing market share, expanding product lines, or opening new locations.

Once the vision and mission are clear, it is essential to conduct a thorough analysis of the current financial situation. This involves reviewing financial statements, such as the balance sheet, income statement, and cash flow statement, to understand the business's financial health. Key metrics to consider include revenue, expenses, profit margins, cash flow, and debt levels. By assessing these metrics, entrepreneurs can identify strengths, weaknesses, and areas for improvement. For Jane, this might mean recognizing that while her bakery's revenue is growing, her profit margins are shrinking due to rising ingredient costs.

With a clear understanding of the current financial situation, the next step is to set specific, measurable, achievable, relevant, and time-bound (SMART) financial goals. Specific goals provide a clear focus, measurable goals allow tracking progress, achievable goals ensure feasibility, relevant goals align with the business's vision and mission, and time-bound goals create a sense of urgency. For instance, rather than setting a vague goal like "increase sales," Jane might set a SMART goal to "increase monthly sales by 15% within the next six months by launching a new line of gluten-free products."

To achieve financial goals, it is crucial to develop a detailed action plan that outlines the steps required to reach each goal. This plan should include specific tasks, responsible individuals, deadlines, and necessary resources. For Jane, the action plan to increase sales might involve conducting market research to identify demand for gluten-free products, sourcing high-quality gluten-free ingredients, training staff on new recipes, and launching a targeted marketing campaign. By breaking down the goal into manageable tasks, Jane can ensure that each step is executed effectively and on time.

Monitoring progress and adjusting the action plan as needed is vital for staying on track. Regularly reviewing financial performance against the set goals helps identify any deviations and allows for timely interventions. Jane might set up monthly review meetings to assess sales data, gather feedback from customers, and evaluate the effectiveness of her marketing efforts. If sales are not increasing as expected, she can adjust her strategy, perhaps by offering promotions or expanding her marketing efforts to reach a broader audience.

One of the common challenges in setting financial goals is balancing short-term needs with long-term aspirations. Short-term goals focus on immediate priorities, such as improving cash flow or reducing expenses, while long-term goals aim at sustaining growth and achieving the business's vision. Jane needs to ensure that her short-term financial decisions do not compromise her long-term objectives. For example, while cutting costs might improve her bakery's short-term profitability, she must avoid compromising the quality of her products, which could damage her brand and hinder long-term growth.

Another critical aspect of setting financial goals is involving the entire team. Engaging employees in the goal-setting process fosters a sense of ownership and accountability. Jane can hold brainstorming sessions with her team to gather ideas, set collective goals, and assign responsibilities. When employees understand how their roles contribute to the business's financial objectives, they are more motivated to perform at their best. Additionally, involving the team in goal-setting helps identify potential challenges and opportunities from different perspectives, leading to more comprehensive and realistic goals.

To support the achievement of financial goals, it is essential to leverage technology and financial tools. Accounting software, budgeting tools, and financial analytics platforms can streamline financial management, provide real-time insights, and facilitate data-driven decision-making. Jane can use these tools

to automate bookkeeping, track expenses, generate
financial reports, and analyze performance metrics.
By utilizing technology, she can save time, reduce
errors, and gain a deeper understanding of her
bakery's financial dynamics.

Setting financial goals also involves anticipating and
managing risks. Every business faces uncertainties,
such as market fluctuations, economic downturns, or
unexpected expenses. By conducting a risk
assessment, Jane can identify potential risks, evaluate
their impact, and develop contingency plans. For
instance, she might create a cash reserve to cover
unforeseen costs or diversify her product offerings to
mitigate the risk of declining demand for a specific
product. Proactive risk management ensures that the
business remains resilient and can adapt to changing
circumstances.

Effective communication is another key element in
setting and achieving financial goals. Transparent
communication with stakeholders, including
employees, investors, and customers, builds trust and
fosters a collaborative environment. Jane should
regularly communicate her bakery's financial goals,
progress, and any challenges faced. This can be done
through team meetings, newsletters, or financial
reports. Clear communication ensures that everyone
is aligned and working towards the same objectives,
and it also provides an opportunity to celebrate
successes and address any concerns.

In addition to setting financial goals, it is important to
continuously invest in professional development.
Staying informed about industry trends, financial best
practices, and emerging technologies can provide

valuable insights and enhance decision-making. Jane can attend workshops, read industry publications, and network with other entrepreneurs to stay updated. By continuously learning and adapting, she can ensure that her bakery remains competitive and well-positioned to achieve its financial goals.

Finally, it is essential to celebrate milestones and achievements along the way. Recognizing and rewarding progress boosts morale, reinforces positive behaviors, and motivates the team to keep striving towards the goals. Jane can celebrate by acknowledging individual contributions, hosting team events, or offering bonuses for meeting targets. Celebrating successes creates a positive and motivating work environment, fostering a culture of achievement and continuous improvement.

Setting financial goals is not a one-time activity but an ongoing process. As the business evolves, financial goals need to be reviewed and adjusted to reflect changing circumstances and new opportunities. Regularly revisiting and refining goals ensures that they remain relevant and aligned with the business's strategic direction. For Jane, this might mean setting new goals to expand her bakery's online presence or exploring new markets. By maintaining a dynamic approach to goal-setting, she can navigate the ever-changing business landscape and achieve sustained success.

In conclusion, setting financial goals is a fundamental practice for any entrepreneur seeking to build a successful and sustainable business. By defining a clear vision, conducting a thorough financial analysis, setting SMART goals, developing detailed action plans, and continuously monitoring progress, entrepreneurs can ensure that their businesses remain focused, resilient, and positioned for long-term growth. Engaging the team, leveraging technology, managing risks, and investing in professional development further support the achievement of financial goals. Through diligent goal-setting and execution, entrepreneurs can turn their visions into reality and achieve lasting success. Achieving financial goals is an iterative journey that requires perseverance, adaptability, and strategic foresight. As entrepreneurs navigate this journey, they must be prepared to encounter obstacles and seize opportunities that arise along the way. One such opportunity lies in fostering strong relationships with key stakeholders, such as suppliers, customers, and financial partners. Building and maintaining these relationships can provide the support and resources necessary to achieve financial objectives.

Building a Financial Mindset

Building a financial mindset is essential for anyone looking to achieve long-term success in business and personal finance. It involves cultivating a set of beliefs, attitudes, and habits that enable individuals to make sound financial decisions, manage resources effectively, and pursue their economic goals with confidence. Developing this mindset requires a combination of self-awareness, education, discipline, and a proactive approach to financial planning.

One of the first steps in building a financial mindset is to understand the importance of financial literacy.

Financial literacy involves having a basic understanding of financial principles, such as budgeting, saving, investing, and debt management. It empowers individuals to make informed decisions about their money and helps them avoid common financial pitfalls. For instance, by understanding the concept of compound interest, one can appreciate the benefits of starting to save early and the impact of long-term investments.

To enhance financial literacy, it is beneficial to seek out educational resources and opportunities. Reading books, attending workshops, and enrolling in online courses can provide valuable knowledge and insights. Engaging with financial news and staying updated on economic trends also helps in making informed decisions. For example, understanding how inflation affects purchasing power can guide investment choices and savings strategies.

Another critical aspect of building a financial mindset is setting clear financial goals. Goals provide direction and motivation, making it easier to stay focused and disciplined. These goals should be specific, measurable, achievable, relevant, and time-bound (SMART). For instance, instead of having a vague goal like "save more money," one might set a goal to "save $10,000 for an emergency fund within the next 12 months." This clarity helps in tracking progress and making necessary adjustments along the way.

A financial mindset also requires the development of disciplined habits. Budgeting is one such habit that is fundamental to financial success. Creating a budget involves tracking income and expenses, identifying areas where money can be saved, and allocating funds towards financial goals. By sticking to a budget, individuals can avoid unnecessary spending and ensure that their resources are being used effectively. For example, by analyzing monthly expenses, one might find that cutting down on dining out can free up funds for savings or investments.

Saving is another crucial habit that supports a strong financial mindset. Building an emergency fund, which typically covers three to six months of living expenses, provides a safety net for unexpected financial challenges. Additionally, saving for specific goals, such as buying a home, funding education, or planning for retirement, ensures that one is prepared for future needs. Automating savings by setting up regular transfers to a savings account can make this process easier and more consistent.

Investing is a key component of building wealth and achieving financial independence. A financial mindset involves understanding the different types of investments, their risks, and potential returns. Diversifying investments across various asset classes, such as stocks, bonds, real estate, and mutual funds, can help manage risk and maximize returns. For instance, investing in a mix of conservative and aggressive assets can balance the portfolio and provide stability during market fluctuations.

Debt management is another important aspect of a financial mindset. While some debt, such as a mortgage or student loans, can be considered an investment in one's future, high-interest consumer debt can be detrimental to financial health. Developing a strategy to pay off debt, prioritizing high-interest debt first, and avoiding unnecessary borrowing are crucial steps. For example, using the debt snowball method, where smaller debts are paid off first to build momentum, can be an effective approach to becoming debt-free.

Mindfulness and self-control play a significant role in building a financial mindset. Being mindful of spending habits and recognizing the difference between needs and wants can prevent impulsive purchases and overspending. Practicing self-control, especially in a consumer-driven society, helps in maintaining financial discipline. For instance, setting a 24-hour rule before making non-essential purchases can provide time to evaluate if the expense is truly necessary.

A positive attitude towards money and wealth is also essential in developing a financial mindset. Viewing money as a tool that enables one to achieve goals and improve quality of life fosters a healthy relationship with finances. This perspective helps in making proactive and intentional financial decisions. For example, instead of seeing saving as a sacrifice, one can view it as a means to secure financial freedom and future opportunities.

Cultivating a growth mindset, the belief that abilities and intelligence can be developed through dedication and hard work, is beneficial for financial success. Embracing challenges, learning from failures, and continually seeking improvement are characteristics of a growth mindset. In financial terms, this means being open to learning new strategies, adapting to changing circumstances, and not being discouraged by setbacks. For instance, if an investment performs poorly, analyzing the reasons and learning from the experience can lead to better decisions in the future.

Networking and seeking advice from financial mentors or advisors can provide valuable guidance and support. Engaging with a community of like-minded individuals who are also focused on financial growth can offer motivation, accountability, and new insights. Attending financial seminars, joining online forums, or participating in investment clubs are ways to build a supportive network. For example, a mentor who has successfully navigated the stock market can provide practical advice and tips for making informed investment choices.

Regularly reviewing and adjusting financial plans is crucial in maintaining a financial mindset. Life circumstances, economic conditions, and personal goals can change over time, necessitating updates to financial strategies. Conducting periodic reviews ensures that financial plans remain relevant and aligned with current objectives. For instance, reassessing investment portfolios annually to ensure they align with risk tolerance and financial goals can lead to more effective financial management.

Building a financial mindset also involves understanding and managing financial stress. Financial challenges can be a significant source of stress, impacting overall well-being. Developing coping strategies, such as maintaining an emergency fund, having a clear financial plan, and seeking professional advice, can help manage stress. Additionally, practicing mindfulness and stress-relief techniques, such as meditation or exercise, can improve mental resilience and decision-making.

Gratitude and generosity are often overlooked aspects of a financial mindset. Practicing gratitude for what one has can shift focus from financial worries to financial well-being. Generosity, through charitable giving or supporting others, fosters a positive relationship with money and can provide a sense of fulfillment. For example, setting aside a portion of income for charitable donations can enhance one's sense of purpose and community involvement.

Ultimately, building a financial mindset is an ongoing journey that requires commitment, education, and adaptability. It involves setting clear goals, developing disciplined habits, and maintaining a positive and proactive approach to financial management. By continuously learning, seeking support, and adjusting plans as needed, individuals can achieve financial stability, growth, and success. This mindset not only improves financial health but also enhances overall quality of life, providing the foundation for achieving personal and professional aspirations. A crucial part of fostering a financial mindset is understanding the impact of personal values and beliefs on financial decisions. Our upbringing, cultural background, and personal experiences shape how we perceive and handle money. Reflecting on these influences can provide clarity and help in aligning financial behaviors with personal values. For instance, someone who values security might prioritize building a robust emergency fund and investing in low-risk assets, while someone who values growth and opportunity might focus on more aggressive investment strategies.

Chapter 2

Budgeting and Financial Planning

Creating a Business Budget

Creating a business budget is a foundational task for any entrepreneur or business owner. It serves as a financial roadmap, guiding decisions, managing resources, and ensuring the business remains viable and profitable. By planning and controlling finances effectively, a budget helps prevent overspending, identifies potential financial problems early, and supports strategic growth.

The first step in creating a business budget is to gather all necessary financial information. This includes historical financial data, such as income statements, balance sheets, and cash flow statements. For a new business, projections based on market research and industry standards can be used. Having a clear understanding of past performance and future expectations is crucial for accurate budgeting.

Once the financial data is gathered, the next step is to estimate revenues. Revenue estimation involves forecasting the sales of goods or services over a specific period, typically a month, quarter, or year. This requires a realistic assessment of market conditions, customer demand, pricing strategies, and competitive landscape. For example, a retail business might analyze past sales trends, seasonal fluctuations, and upcoming marketing campaigns to project future sales.

After estimating revenues, it's essential to identify and categorize expenses. Expenses can be divided into fixed and variable costs. Fixed costs, such as rent, salaries, and insurance, remain constant regardless of business activity levels. Variable costs, including raw materials, utilities, and sales commissions, fluctuate with production and sales volume. Understanding these distinctions helps in managing and controlling expenses more effectively.

A detailed list of all expenses should be created, categorized, and prioritized. This includes both direct costs, like materials and labor directly tied to production, and indirect costs, such as administrative expenses and marketing. For instance, a manufacturing business would list costs for raw materials, production labor, factory overhead, and distribution, while also accounting for indirect costs like office supplies and advertising.

With estimated revenues and identified expenses, the next step is to create a profit and loss statement (P&L). A P&L statement, also known as an income statement, summarizes the projected revenues, expenses, and profits over a specific period. This statement helps in understanding the expected financial performance and identifying areas that need adjustment. For example, if projected expenses exceed revenues, it may be necessary to cut costs, increase prices, or find new revenue streams.

Cash flow management is another critical aspect of business budgeting. Cash flow refers to the inflow and outflow of cash in a business. Even profitable businesses can face challenges if cash flow is not managed properly. Creating a cash flow statement helps in tracking the timing of cash receipts and payments, ensuring that the business has enough liquidity to meet its obligations. For instance, a business might have high sales but face cash flow issues if customers delay payments. Planning for such scenarios by maintaining a cash reserve or arranging short-term financing can prevent cash flow crises.

Budgeting for contingencies is also important. Unexpected expenses and emergencies can disrupt financial plans. Setting aside a contingency fund, typically a percentage of total expenses, provides a buffer for unforeseen costs. For example, a business might allocate 5-10% of its budget for contingencies to cover unexpected repairs, legal fees, or market changes.

Regular monitoring and reviewing of the budget are essential for its effectiveness. A budget is not a static document but a dynamic tool that needs to be updated and adjusted as circumstances change. Monthly or quarterly reviews help in comparing actual performance with budgeted figures, identifying variances, and taking corrective actions. For instance, if marketing expenses are higher than budgeted, a business can analyze the reasons and adjust future spending accordingly.

Involving key stakeholders in the budgeting process enhances its accuracy and buy-in. Engaging department heads, managers, and other relevant personnel ensures that all aspects of the business are considered and that there is a shared understanding of financial goals and constraints. Collaborative budgeting fosters accountability and promotes a culture of financial responsibility. For example, a sales manager's input on revenue forecasts and market trends can provide valuable insights for more accurate budgeting.

Using budgeting software or tools can streamline the process and improve accuracy. Many software options are available, ranging from simple spreadsheets to advanced financial management systems. These tools can automate calculations, provide templates, and generate detailed financial reports, making it easier to create and manage budgets. For instance, software like QuickBooks or Xero offers features for tracking expenses, forecasting revenues, and analyzing financial performance.

Scenario planning is another useful technique in business budgeting. By creating different budget scenarios based on various assumptions, businesses can prepare for different outcomes and develop strategies to mitigate risks. For example, a business might create best-case, worst-case, and most-likely scenarios to understand the potential impact of changes in sales volume, cost fluctuations, or economic conditions. This approach helps in making informed decisions and being better prepared for uncertainties.

Incorporating performance metrics and key performance indicators (KPIs) into the budget can provide additional insights and help in monitoring progress. KPIs, such as gross profit margin, operating margin, and return on investment, offer measurable targets that align with financial goals. Tracking these metrics regularly helps in assessing financial health and identifying areas for improvement. For instance, a business might set a KPI for reducing operating expenses by a certain percentage over the next year and monitor progress through monthly budget reviews.

Effective communication of the budget to the entire team is crucial for its successful implementation. Ensuring that all employees understand the budget, its goals, and their role in achieving them fosters a sense of ownership and accountability. Regular updates and transparent communication about financial performance and any changes to the budget keep everyone aligned and motivated. For example, sharing quarterly budget reports and discussing results in team meetings can reinforce the importance of financial discipline and collective effort.

Continuous learning and improvement are vital for refining the budgeting process. Seeking feedback from stakeholders, analyzing the effectiveness of past budgets, and staying informed about industry best practices can lead to better budgeting practices over time. For instance, attending financial management workshops, reading relevant literature, or consulting with financial experts can provide new insights and techniques for more efficient budgeting.

In conclusion, creating a business budget is a comprehensive process that involves gathering financial data, estimating revenues, identifying and categorizing expenses, and regularly monitoring and adjusting the budget. It requires collaboration, effective communication, and continuous learning to ensure its accuracy and relevance. By following these principles and practices, businesses can achieve financial stability, make informed decisions, and pursue strategic growth with confidence. A well-constructed budget not only guides day-to-day operations but also serves as a strategic tool for long-term success, providing a clear financial framework for achieving business objectives. In addition to the core steps of creating a business budget, there are several advanced strategies and considerations that can further enhance financial planning and management. One such strategy is zero-based budgeting (ZBB). Unlike traditional budgeting, which often adjusts previous budgets incrementally, ZBB starts from a "zero base" each period. Every expense must be justified and approved, rather than simply carried over. This method can lead to more efficient allocation of resources and eliminate outdated or unnecessary expenditures. For instance, if a department has been receiving a fixed budget year after year, ZBB would require it to justify every dollar spent, potentially uncovering savings opportunities.

Short-term vs. Long-term Planning

Balancing short-term and long-term planning is crucial for the success and sustainability of any business. Both approaches serve distinct purposes but must work in harmony to ensure immediate needs are met without compromising future goals.
Understanding the nuances of each type of planning and how to effectively integrate them is essential for business leaders.

Short-term planning typically focuses on the immediate future, covering a period ranging from a few months up to a year. This type of planning deals with day-to-day operations, cash flow management, and immediate business needs. For instance, a retailer might plan for inventory purchases ahead of the holiday season, ensuring they have enough stock to meet customer demand. Short-term plans are often more detailed and specific, addressing operational tasks such as marketing campaigns, staffing schedules, and budget allocations for the upcoming quarter.

One of the primary benefits of short-term planning is its ability to provide quick feedback and allow for rapid adjustments. Businesses can respond to market changes, customer preferences, and competitive pressures in real time. For example, a tech company might launch a new product and, based on early sales data and customer feedback, quickly iterate and improve the product or its marketing strategy. This agility is essential in fast-paced industries where conditions can change rapidly.

However, short-term planning also has its limitations. Focusing too heavily on immediate concerns can lead to a reactive rather than proactive approach, potentially neglecting long-term goals and sustainability. Businesses that prioritize short-term gains, such as cutting costs at the expense of quality, may find themselves struggling with customer dissatisfaction and brand damage in the long run. It's akin to sprinting in a marathon; while it might give a temporary lead, it's unsustainable over the long haul.

Long-term planning, on the other hand, involves setting goals and strategies that span several years, often five to ten years into the future. This type of planning is strategic and visionary, defining the overall direction and aspirations of the business. A manufacturing company, for example, might set a long-term goal to reduce its carbon footprint by 50% over the next decade, requiring investments in new technologies and processes. Long-term plans encompass broader objectives like market expansion, product diversification, and building core competencies.

The advantage of long-term planning lies in its ability to provide a clear vision and direction for the business. It encourages strategic thinking, innovation, and investment in initiatives that may not yield immediate returns but are critical for sustained growth and competitiveness. For instance, a pharmaceutical company investing in research and development might not see profits from a new drug for several years, but this investment is essential for future breakthroughs and maintaining a competitive edge.

However, the challenge with long-term planning is the inherent uncertainty and the difficulty of predicting future conditions. Economic shifts, technological advancements, and changes in consumer behavior can all impact the feasibility and relevance of long-term plans. Therefore, it's important for long-term plans to be flexible and adaptable, allowing businesses to pivot as necessary while staying true to their overarching vision.

Integrating short-term and long-term planning requires a balanced approach that aligns immediate actions with future objectives. One effective strategy is to use short-term goals as stepping stones toward long-term aspirations. For instance, a company aiming to double its market share in five years might set annual targets for incremental growth, each supported by specific short-term initiatives like marketing campaigns, product launches, and customer engagement programs.

Regularly reviewing and adjusting both short-term and long-term plans is also crucial. Businesses should establish a routine of quarterly or bi-annual reviews to assess progress, identify any deviations, and make necessary adjustments. This dynamic approach ensures that short-term actions remain aligned with long-term goals, and that both can adapt to changing circumstances. For example, a company might find that a new competitor has entered the market, requiring a shift in both immediate tactics and long-term strategies.

Communication and collaboration across all levels of the organization are vital for successful integration. Ensuring that everyone, from executives to frontline employees, understands the company's long-term vision and how their daily tasks contribute to these goals fosters a cohesive and motivated workforce. For instance, regular town hall meetings and transparent updates on both short-term achievements and long-term strategies can help maintain alignment and morale.

Utilizing tools and frameworks can also enhance the integration of short-term and long-term planning. The

Balanced Scorecard, for instance, allows businesses to set and track performance metrics across multiple perspectives—financial, customer, internal processes, and learning and growth. This holistic approach ensures that short-term efforts contribute to long-term success. A tech startup might use this framework to balance immediate revenue targets with long-term innovation and customer satisfaction goals.

Scenario planning is another valuable tool. By developing and analyzing different future scenarios, businesses can prepare for a range of possibilities and ensure that both short-term and long-term plans are robust and flexible. For example, a global retailer might create scenarios based on various economic conditions, regulatory changes, and technological advancements, allowing them to develop strategies that are resilient to different future states.

Investing in talent and leadership development is essential for bridging short-term and long-term planning. Leaders who can think strategically and act tactically are valuable assets. They ensure that daily operations and immediate goals are pursued with an eye towards the future. For example, a company might implement leadership training programs that emphasize both strategic vision and operational excellence, preparing managers to navigate short-term challenges while keeping long-term objectives in focus.

Finally, fostering a culture of innovation can help balance short-term execution with long-term exploration. Encouraging employees to experiment, take calculated risks, and propose new ideas can lead to breakthroughs that drive both immediate improvements and future growth. For instance, a software company might allocate a portion of its budget to innovation labs or hackathons, where employees can work on creative projects that align with the company's strategic goals.

In conclusion, balancing short-term and long-term planning is a dynamic and ongoing process that requires careful consideration, strategic alignment, and continuous adaptation. By understanding the distinct purposes and benefits of each type of planning, and by integrating them effectively, businesses can navigate immediate challenges while building a sustainable and prosperous future. Embracing tools, fostering a culture of innovation, and investing in leadership development are key to achieving this balance, ensuring that short-term actions support long-term success and that the organization remains agile and resilient in a constantly changing environment.

Financial Forecasting

Financial forecasting is the bedrock of sound business planning, enabling organizations to anticipate future financial conditions and make strategic decisions. It involves predicting future revenues, expenses, and capital needs based on historical data, market analysis, and economic trends. For beginners, mastering financial forecasting can seem daunting, but with the right approach and tools, it becomes a powerful asset in guiding business growth and stability.

At its core, financial forecasting begins with a thorough understanding of the company's historical performance. This involves collecting and analyzing data from financial statements—income statements, balance sheets, and cash flow statements. By examining past trends in revenue, expenses, and profit margins, businesses can identify patterns and use them as a baseline for future projections. For instance, a retail company might notice that its sales peak during the holiday season, which can inform forecasts for inventory purchases and staffing needs.

Once historical data is analyzed, businesses should consider external factors that could impact their financial future. Economic indicators such as inflation rates, unemployment rates, and GDP growth are crucial as they influence consumer spending and business investment. Additionally, industry-specific trends and competitive analysis provide insights into potential shifts in market demand and pricing strategies. For example, a tech company might track advancements in technology and competitor product launches to forecast its own sales and R&D expenditures.

There are several methods of financial forecasting, each with its own strengths and applications. The most commonly used methods include qualitative forecasting, time series analysis, and causal models. Qualitative forecasting relies on expert judgment and market research. This method is particularly useful for new businesses without extensive historical data. For instance, a startup might use surveys and expert opinions to estimate its market potential and forecast initial sales.

Time series analysis uses historical data to identify trends, cycles, and seasonal patterns. This statistical method is valuable for businesses with consistent historical performance. By applying techniques such as moving averages or exponential smoothing, companies can project future values based on past behaviors. For example, a restaurant might use time series analysis to predict monthly revenue, accounting for seasonal variations and special events.

Causal models, on the other hand, establish cause-and-effect relationships between variables. These models consider external factors that influence financial outcomes, such as marketing spend, economic conditions, and competitive actions. By using regression analysis, businesses can quantify the impact of these variables on their financial performance. For instance, an e-commerce company might develop a causal model to forecast sales based on advertising expenditures and website traffic.

A critical aspect of financial forecasting is scenario analysis, which involves creating multiple projections based on different assumptions. This approach helps businesses prepare for various potential future states and develop contingency plans. For example, a manufacturing company might create best-case, worst-case, and most-likely scenarios for its sales forecasts, considering factors like supply chain disruptions, changes in raw material costs, and shifts in customer demand. Scenario analysis enables businesses to identify risks and opportunities, making them more resilient in the face of uncertainty.

Cash flow forecasting is another vital component of financial forecasting. It focuses on predicting the inflows and outflows of cash to ensure the business can meet its financial obligations. A positive cash flow is essential for day-to-day operations, paying suppliers, and investing in growth opportunities. Businesses should monitor their cash flow regularly and adjust their forecasts based on actual performance. For instance, a service company might forecast its cash flow by analyzing expected client payments and upcoming expenses, ensuring it maintains sufficient liquidity.

Financial forecasting is not a one-time activity but an ongoing process that requires regular updates and adjustments. Businesses should establish a routine for reviewing and revising their forecasts, incorporating new data and insights as they become available. This iterative approach ensures that forecasts remain accurate and relevant, enabling the business to adapt to changing conditions. For example, a retail chain might update its sales forecasts monthly, incorporating actual sales data and adjusting for promotional campaigns and market trends.

One of the key challenges in financial forecasting is dealing with uncertainty and variability. No forecast can be entirely accurate, and unexpected events can significantly impact financial outcomes. To mitigate this risk, businesses should adopt a conservative approach, using realistic assumptions and building in buffers for unforeseen circumstances. For instance, a construction company might include contingency funds in its project forecasts to account for potential delays or cost overruns.

Technology plays a crucial role in enhancing the accuracy and efficiency of financial forecasting.

Advanced software tools and analytics platforms enable businesses to automate data collection, perform complex analyses, and generate detailed forecasts. These tools often include features like scenario modeling, trend analysis, and visualization, making it easier for businesses to interpret and communicate their forecasts. For example, a financial software platform might allow a company to input various assumptions and instantly generate multiple forecast scenarios, helping decision-makers understand the potential impacts of different strategies.

Effective communication of financial forecasts is essential for gaining buy-in from stakeholders and guiding strategic decision-making. Businesses should present their forecasts clearly and concisely, highlighting key assumptions, methodologies, and potential risks. Visual aids like charts and graphs can help convey complex data in an understandable format. For instance, a CFO might present the company's financial forecast to the board of directors using a combination of detailed reports and visual summaries, facilitating informed discussions and decisions.

Financial forecasting also has implications for strategic planning and performance management. By aligning forecasts with business goals, companies can set realistic targets and measure their progress over time. For example, a company aiming to expand its market share might use its sales forecasts to set quarterly revenue targets and track its performance against these benchmarks. This alignment helps ensure that the company stays on track to achieve its long-term objectives while making necessary adjustments along the way.

Training and development are important for building forecasting capabilities within an organization. Employees involved in the forecasting process should have a strong understanding of financial principles, analytical techniques, and the specific dynamics of their industry. Providing training and resources, such as workshops and online courses, can enhance their skills and improve the accuracy of forecasts. For example, a company might offer financial modeling training to its finance team, equipping them with advanced techniques for developing robust forecasts.

Incorporating feedback loops into the forecasting process is another best practice. By comparing actual performance against forecasts, businesses can identify areas for improvement and refine their forecasting models. This continuous feedback helps enhance the accuracy of future forecasts and improves decision-making. For instance, a marketing team might analyze the variance between forecasted and actual campaign results, using the insights to adjust their future marketing spend and strategies.

In conclusion, financial forecasting is an indispensable tool for business planning and decision-making. By understanding historical data, considering external factors, and employing various forecasting methods, businesses can anticipate future financial conditions and make informed strategic choices. Regular updates, scenario analysis, and effective communication further enhance the value of financial forecasts. As businesses navigate the complexities of the market, robust financial forecasting provides the foresight needed to achieve sustainable growth and success. Moreover, integrating financial forecasting into the broader strategic framework of the organization ensures that it is not just a standalone activity but a vital part of the business's overall planning and management process. This holistic approach helps align financial goals with operational strategies, ensuring that every department works towards common objectives. For instance, a manufacturing company might integrate its sales forecasts with its production planning, ensuring that output levels meet anticipated demand without leading to excess inventory or stockouts.

Managing Unexpected Expenses

Every business, regardless of its size or industry, will inevitably face unexpected expenses. These unanticipated costs can stem from a myriad of sources: equipment failures, emergency repairs, legal issues, or even sudden market changes. Effectively managing these expenses is crucial to maintaining financial stability and ensuring long-term success. By developing a proactive strategy, businesses can cushion the impact of unforeseen costs and navigate financial turbulence with greater confidence.

One of the first steps in managing unexpected expenses is to establish a robust emergency fund. This fund acts as a financial safety net, providing immediate access to cash when unforeseen expenses arise. Ideally, the emergency fund should cover three to six months of operating expenses, though the exact amount can vary based on the business's risk profile and industry. For example, a manufacturing company with expensive machinery might require a larger emergency fund compared to a consultancy firm with minimal overhead costs. Building this fund requires discipline and foresight, often involving setting aside a portion of monthly revenues until the desired amount is reached.

In addition to an emergency fund, maintaining a line of credit can offer businesses additional financial flexibility. A line of credit provides access to funds that can be drawn upon as needed, without the immediate obligation to repay. This can be particularly useful for covering large, unexpected expenses that exceed the available emergency fund. For instance, if a retail business faces an unexpected spike in inventory costs due to supply chain disruptions, it can use its line of credit to cover the shortfall without disrupting daily operations. Businesses should establish lines of credit during stable periods, ensuring they have access to funds before they are urgently needed.

Insurance is another critical component in managing unexpected expenses. Comprehensive insurance policies can protect businesses from a wide range of risks, including property damage, liability claims, and business interruption. Regularly reviewing and updating insurance coverage ensures that the business remains adequately protected as it grows and evolves. For example, a restaurant might need to adjust its insurance coverage as it expands its premises or introduces new services like delivery. Working with an experienced insurance broker can help businesses identify potential gaps in coverage and secure policies that match their specific needs.

Diversifying revenue streams is a strategic approach that can mitigate the financial impact of unexpected expenses. By generating income from multiple sources, businesses reduce their reliance on a single revenue stream, thereby spreading financial risk. For instance, a software company that offers both one-time license sales and subscription-based services can buffer against unexpected dips in either revenue stream. Diversification can also involve exploring new markets or product lines, which can provide additional financial resilience. However, diversification should be approached cautiously, ensuring that new ventures align with the business's core competencies and strategic goals.

Effective cash flow management is essential for handling unexpected expenses. Businesses should regularly monitor their cash flow to ensure they have sufficient liquidity to meet both anticipated and unanticipated costs. This involves tracking incoming revenues, outgoing expenses, and timing discrepancies between the two. For example, a construction firm might face delayed payments from clients while still needing to pay suppliers and employees on time. By creating detailed cash flow forecasts, businesses can anticipate potential shortfalls and take preemptive measures, such as negotiating extended payment terms with suppliers or accelerating receivables collection.

Cost control is another important aspect of managing unexpected expenses. Regularly reviewing and optimizing operational costs can free up resources that can be redirected towards unexpected needs. This involves analyzing expenses to identify areas where costs can be reduced without compromising quality or efficiency. For example, a company might renegotiate contracts with suppliers, implement energy-saving initiatives, or streamline its workforce to reduce payroll expenses. Cost control should be an ongoing effort, with periodic reviews to identify new opportunities for savings.

Building strong relationships with suppliers and vendors can provide additional support during times of unexpected expenses. Reliable suppliers may be willing to offer flexible payment terms or discounts in response to a long-standing business relationship. For instance, a restaurant facing a sudden spike in ingredient costs might negotiate delayed payments or bulk purchase discounts with its suppliers. Maintaining open communication and fostering mutual trust with suppliers can create a supportive network that businesses can rely on during financial challenges.

Leveraging technology can also play a significant role in managing unexpected expenses. Financial management software can provide real-time insights into the business's financial health, enabling quicker responses to unanticipated costs. These tools can automate expense tracking, generate accurate financial reports, and forecast future cash flow needs. For example, a small business using accounting software can quickly identify unexpected spikes in expenses and adjust its budget accordingly. Investing in such technology can enhance financial agility and improve decision-making processes.

Training and empowering employees to manage resources efficiently can further strengthen a business's ability to handle unexpected expenses. Employees who understand the importance of cost control and resource management can contribute to identifying savings and improving operational efficiency. For example, a team of sales representatives who are trained to manage their travel expenses judiciously can reduce the overall travel budget. Encouraging a culture of financial responsibility across the organization ensures that everyone is aligned in managing costs effectively.

Scenario planning is a proactive technique that prepares businesses for potential unexpected expenses. By envisioning various scenarios and their potential financial impacts, businesses can develop contingency plans and response strategies. This involves identifying key risks, assessing their likelihood and potential impact, and creating action plans for each scenario. For instance, a retail chain might develop scenarios for different levels of sales decline due to economic downturns and outline cost-cutting measures for each scenario. Scenario planning helps businesses remain agile and responsive, reducing the shock of unexpected expenses.

Regular financial health checks are vital for early detection of potential issues that could lead to unexpected expenses. This involves conducting periodic reviews of financial statements, performance metrics, and key financial ratios. For example, a business might track its debt-to-equity ratio to ensure it is not over-leveraged, which could lead to unexpected interest expenses. Identifying and addressing financial red flags early can prevent minor issues from escalating into significant financial burdens.

Lastly, maintaining a positive relationship with financial institutions can provide additional support during times of unexpected expenses. Banks and lenders are more likely to offer favorable terms and support to businesses with a strong track record of financial responsibility and transparent communication. For instance, a business that regularly updates its bank on its financial performance and strategic plans may find it easier to secure a short-term loan during a financial crunch. Building and maintaining these relationships requires consistent communication, timely repayments, and a clear demonstration of financial stewardship.

In summary, managing unexpected expenses requires a multifaceted approach that includes building financial reserves, maintaining access to credit, securing comprehensive insurance, diversifying revenue streams, and optimizing cash flow management. By fostering strong supplier relationships, leveraging technology, empowering employees, and engaging in scenario planning, businesses can enhance their financial resilience. Regular financial health checks and positive relationships with financial institutions further support the ability to navigate unforeseen costs. Through these strategies, businesses can not only manage unexpected expenses effectively but also strengthen their overall financial stability and ensure long-term success. Additionally, a disciplined budgeting process is fundamental to preparing for unexpected expenses. Creating a flexible budget that includes a contingency fund for unforeseen expenditures can help absorb financial shocks. This involves setting realistic financial goals, tracking expenses meticulously, and adjusting the budget as needed throughout the fiscal year. For example, a tech startup might allocate a portion of its budget to a contingency fund, which can be used to cover unexpected costs like emergency server maintenance or legal fees.

Adjusting Budgets for Business Growth

Growth is an exhilarating phase for any business; it signifies that the company is moving in the right direction, capturing more market share, and increasing its revenue. However, with growth comes a set of financial challenges that need meticulous planning and adjustment, especially in terms of budgeting. Budgeting for business growth involves not just scaling up operations but also anticipating and managing the financial demands that come with expansion. This chapter delves into the essential strategies for adjusting budgets to accommodate and sustain business growth effectively.

The first step in adjusting a budget for growth is to reassess the business's financial goals and objectives. Growth typically requires a significant investment in various areas such as infrastructure, human resources, marketing, and technology. Therefore, it's crucial to revisit and possibly redefine financial goals to align them with the new growth trajectory. For instance, if a business plans to expand its market presence, it might set a financial goal to increase its marketing budget by 20% over the next year. Clearly defined goals provide a roadmap for allocating resources efficiently and measuring progress.

One of the most critical areas that demand attention during growth is cash flow management. Growth often entails increased expenses before the revenue catches up, leading to potential cash flow challenges. To mitigate this, businesses should create detailed cash flow forecasts that account for the expected increases in both expenses and revenue. For example, a retail business anticipating a surge in sales during the holiday season should forecast the additional cash required for inventory purchases and staffing. Regularly updating these forecasts helps in identifying potential cash shortfalls early and taking corrective actions such as securing short-term financing or adjusting payment terms with suppliers.

Investing in technology is another pivotal aspect of budgeting for growth. As businesses expand, they often need to upgrade their technology infrastructure to support increased operations. This can include investing in new software, upgrading existing systems, or even overhauling the entire IT infrastructure. For example, a growing e-commerce platform might need to invest in a more robust server infrastructure to handle increased traffic and transactions. While these investments can be substantial, they are essential for maintaining operational efficiency and providing a better customer experience. Allocating a portion of the budget for technology upgrades ensures that the business can scale without facing operational bottlenecks. resources also play a significant role in supporting business growth. Expanding operations often means hiring additional staff or upskilling existing employees to meet the new demands. This requires careful planning and budgeting for recruitment, training, and salaries. For instance, a tech startup experiencing rapid growth might need to hire additional developers and customer support staff. Budgeting for these new hires involves not only their salaries but also recruitment costs, onboarding expenses, and potential training programs. Additionally, offering competitive compensation packages is crucial for attracting and retaining top talent in a competitive market.

Marketing and advertising budgets typically need to be adjusted during periods of growth. Expanding into new markets or increasing market share in existing ones requires a more aggressive marketing strategy. This might involve increased spending on digital marketing campaigns, social media advertising, content creation, and other promotional activities. For example, a company launching a new product line might allocate a significant portion of its budget to a comprehensive marketing campaign to create awareness and drive sales. It's essential to monitor the return on investment (ROI) of these marketing efforts to ensure that the increased spending is translating into tangible business results.

Inventory management is another area that requires careful budgeting during growth. Increased sales volumes often necessitate higher inventory levels to meet customer demand. This involves not only the cost of purchasing additional inventory but also storage and logistics costs. For example, a growing online retailer might need to budget for additional warehouse space and enhanced logistics capabilities to ensure timely delivery of products. Effective inventory management and budgeting help in avoiding stockouts or overstocking, both of which can negatively impact cash flow and profitability.

Expanding into new markets or launching new products often comes with regulatory and compliance costs. Businesses need to ensure that they comply with all relevant regulations in the new markets they enter. This might involve legal fees, licensing costs, and other compliance-related expenses. For instance, a food and beverage company expanding into a new country might need to budget for obtaining local health and safety certifications. Understanding and budgeting for these costs upfront prevents compliance issues that could derail growth plans.

Risk management becomes increasingly important as businesses grow. Larger operations and increased market presence expose businesses to a wider range of risks, including market volatility, supply chain disruptions, and competitive pressures. Allocating a portion of the budget for risk management activities, such as purchasing insurance, implementing robust internal controls, and diversifying supply chains, can help mitigate these risks. For example, a manufacturing company expanding its operations might invest in business interruption insurance to protect against potential production halts due to unforeseen circumstances.

Continuous monitoring and adjustment of the budget are crucial during periods of growth. Growth trajectories can be unpredictable, and businesses need to remain agile and responsive to changing circumstances. Regularly reviewing financial performance against the budget allows businesses to identify variances and adjust their plans accordingly. For instance, if a marketing campaign is not delivering the expected results, the business might reallocate those funds to a more effective strategy. This dynamic approach to budgeting ensures that resources are always aligned with the most critical growth initiatives.

Engaging stakeholders in the budgeting process is vital for ensuring that all aspects of the business are considered and adequately funded. This includes involving department heads, financial advisors, and even key customers or suppliers in the planning process. For example, a company planning to launch a new product might involve its sales team to gather insights on market demand and customer preferences. This collaborative approach helps in creating a more accurate and comprehensive budget that supports the overall growth strategy.

Lastly, maintaining a balance between short-term needs and long-term goals is essential when adjusting budgets for growth. While it's important to address immediate financial needs, businesses should not lose sight of their long-term vision and objectives. This involves making strategic investments that might not yield immediate returns but are crucial for sustaining growth in the long run. For instance, investing in research and development (R&D) to innovate new products can be a significant expense but is essential for staying competitive in the market.

In summary, adjusting budgets for business growth requires a holistic and strategic approach. It involves reassessing financial goals, managing cash flow, investing in technology and human resources, enhancing marketing efforts, and maintaining effective inventory management. Additionally, businesses need to account for regulatory costs, manage risks, continuously monitor and adjust budgets, engage stakeholders, and balance short-term needs with long-term goals. By adopting these strategies, businesses can effectively manage the financial demands of growth and ensure sustainable success. Navigating the complexities of budgeting during growth also involves leveraging financial data and analytics. Detailed financial analysis can provide valuable insights into the areas where the business is performing well and where adjustments might be necessary. For instance, analyzing profit margins across different product lines can highlight which products are driving growth and which ones are lagging. This information can then inform decisions on where to allocate additional resources or where cost-cutting measures might be appropriate.

Chapter 3

Understanding Financial Statements

The Balance Sheet

A balance sheet is one of the fundamental financial statements essential for understanding a company's financial position at a specific point in time. It's a snapshot that provides insights into what the company owns, what it owes, and the shareholders' equity. For beginners, mastering the balance sheet is crucial because it lays the groundwork for deeper financial analysis and decision-making.

The balance sheet is structured into three main sections: assets, liabilities, and shareholders' equity. Each of these sections plays a vital role in painting a comprehensive picture of the company's financial health.

Assets are resources owned by the company that have economic value and can be converted into cash. They are typically categorized into current and non-current assets. Current assets include cash, accounts receivable, inventory, and other resources expected to be converted into cash within a year. For instance, a retail company might have significant amounts of inventory ready for sale, which is considered a current asset. Non-current assets, on the other hand, are long-term investments that provide value over time, such as property, plant, equipment, and intangible assets like patents and trademarks.

Cash is the most liquid asset and is vital for day-to-day operations. A strong cash position indicates that the company can meet its short-term obligations and invest in opportunities as they arise. Accounts receivable represent money owed to the company by customers who have purchased goods or services on credit. Efficient management of accounts receivable is crucial because it impacts cash flow. For example, if a company has high accounts receivable but struggles to collect payments, it could face cash flow issues despite having strong sales.

Inventory management is another critical aspect of current assets. Inventory includes raw materials, work-in-progress, and finished goods ready for sale. Effective inventory management ensures that the company maintains the right balance—having enough stock to meet customer demand without tying up excessive capital. For example, a manufacturing company must carefully monitor its inventory levels to avoid production delays or excess holding costs.

Non-current assets, also known as fixed assets, are long-term investments that include property, plant, and equipment (PP&E). These assets are essential for the company's operations and often involve significant capital expenditure. For instance, a technology company might invest heavily in state-of-the-art equipment and research facilities. Over time, these assets depreciate, and the company must account for this depreciation in its financial statements. Depreciation represents the wear and tear on these assets and is crucial for accurately reflecting their value.

Liabilities represent the company's obligations—what it owes to others. Similar to assets, liabilities are divided into current and non-current categories. Current liabilities are obligations that the company must settle within a year, such as accounts payable, short-term loans, and accrued expenses. For example, a company might have accounts payable to suppliers for raw materials purchased on credit. Efficient management of current liabilities is essential to maintain liquidity and creditworthiness.

Non-current liabilities are long-term obligations that extend beyond a year, such as long-term loans, bonds payable, and deferred tax liabilities. For instance, a company might issue bonds to raise capital for expansion projects. These bonds are a form of debt that the company must repay over several years, often with interest. Understanding the company's long-term debt obligations is crucial for assessing its financial stability and ability to meet future commitments.

Shareholders' equity represents the owners' claims on the company's assets after all liabilities have been paid. It includes common stock, retained earnings, and additional paid-in capital. Common stock represents the ownership shares issued to investors. Retained earnings are the accumulated profits that the company has reinvested in the business rather than distributing as dividends. For example, a profitable company might choose to reinvest its earnings into research and development to drive future growth. Additional paid-in capital represents the excess amount investors pay over the par value of the stock.

The balance sheet follows the fundamental accounting equation: Assets = Liabilities + Shareholders' Equity. This equation must always balance, ensuring that the company's resources are funded either by borrowing (liabilities) or by the owners (equity). For instance, if a company purchases equipment for $100,000 using a $60,000 loan and $40,000 in cash, both sides of the equation will balance: the asset side increases by $100,000 (equipment), and the liability side increases by $60,000 (loan) and $40,000 (equity).

Analyzing the balance sheet involves several financial ratios that provide deeper insights into the company's performance and financial health. One such ratio is the current ratio, calculated as current assets divided by current liabilities. This ratio measures the company's ability to meet its short-term obligations with its short-term assets. A current ratio greater than 1 indicates that the company has more current assets than current liabilities, suggesting good liquidity. For example, a current ratio of 1.5 means the company has $1.50 in current assets for every $1.00 in current liabilities.

Another important ratio is the debt-to-equity ratio, calculated as total liabilities divided by shareholders' equity. This ratio measures the company's financial leverage and indicates the proportion of debt used to finance the company's assets relative to the equity. A high debt-to-equity ratio suggests that the company relies heavily on debt financing, which could be risky if it struggles to generate enough cash flow to meet its debt obligations. For instance, a debt-to-equity ratio of 2 means the company has $2 in debt for every $1 in equity.

The return on equity (ROE) ratio is another key metric, calculated as net income divided by shareholders' equity. ROE measures the company's profitability relative to the equity invested by the shareholders. A higher ROE indicates that the company is efficiently using shareholders' equity to generate profits. For example, an ROE of 15% means the company generates $0.15 in profit for every $1 of equity.

Understanding the balance sheet also involves recognizing its limitations. While the balance sheet provides a snapshot of the company's financial position at a specific point in time, it does not capture the company's operational performance over time. Therefore, it is essential to analyze the balance sheet in conjunction with other financial statements, such as the income statement and cash flow statement, to gain a comprehensive understanding of the company's overall financial health.

Moreover, the balance sheet does not account for intangible assets that are difficult to quantify, such as brand reputation, employee expertise, and customer loyalty. These intangible assets can significantly impact the company's long-term success but are not reflected in the balance sheet's figures. For instance, a strong brand like Apple or Coca-Cola has immense value that contributes to the company's market position but is not directly recorded on the balance sheet.

In practice, creating and maintaining an accurate balance sheet requires diligent record-keeping and regular updates. Businesses must ensure that all transactions are recorded correctly and that asset valuations are up-to-date. For example, if a company acquires new equipment, it must update its balance sheet to reflect the new asset and any associated liabilities. Regular audits and reconciliations help maintain the accuracy and reliability of the balance sheet.

For beginners, mastering the balance sheet involves not only understanding its components but also practicing its preparation and analysis. Regularly reviewing and analyzing the balance sheet can provide valuable insights into the company's financial strengths and weaknesses, helping inform strategic decisions. For instance, if the balance sheet reveals high levels of debt, the company might prioritize debt repayment to reduce financial risk.

In summary, the balance sheet is a critical financial statement that provides a snapshot of a company's financial position at a specific point in time. By understanding its components—assets, liabilities, and shareholders' equity—businesses can gain valuable insights into their financial health and make informed decisions. Analyzing key ratios such as the current ratio, debt-to-equity ratio, and return on equity can further enhance this understanding. While the balance sheet has its limitations, it remains an essential tool for financial analysis and strategic planning. Through diligent record-keeping and regular analysis, businesses can leverage the balance sheet to drive growth and long-term success. The balance sheet's role in strategic planning cannot be overstated. It provides a foundation for making informed decisions about investments, financing, and operations. For instance, a company with a strong balance sheet, characterized by substantial assets and minimal liabilities, might be well-positioned to invest in new growth opportunities or weather economic downturns. Conversely, a company with a weaker balance sheet might need to focus on shoring up its financial position before pursuing aggressive growth strategies.

Income Statement

The income statement, also known as the profit and loss statement, is a critical financial document that provides a summary of a company's revenues, expenses, and profits over a specific period. It offers insights into the operational efficiency and profitability of the business, making it a crucial tool for managers, investors, and other stakeholders. For beginners, understanding the income statement is essential for analyzing a company's financial performance and making informed decisions.

The income statement is structured into two main sections: revenues and expenses. Revenues, also known as sales or income, represent the money earned from the company's core business activities. This could include sales of products or services, interest income, royalties, and other sources of income. For example, a retail store's revenue would largely come from the sale of merchandise, while a service-based business might generate revenue from consulting fees.

Revenue is often categorized into operating revenue and non-operating revenue. Operating revenue is derived from the primary activities of the business.

For instance, a manufacturing company's operating revenue would come from selling its products. Non-operating revenue, on the other hand, includes income from secondary activities, such as interest earned on investments or rental income from property owned by the company. Although non-operating revenue can contribute to the overall financial health of a business, it is the operating revenue that provides a clearer picture of the company's core performance.

The next section of the income statement is expenses. Expenses are the costs incurred in generating revenue and running the business. They include cost of goods sold (COGS), operating expenses, and non-operating expenses. COGS refers to the direct costs associated with producing goods or services sold by the company, such as raw materials and labor. For example, in a bakery, the cost of flour, sugar, and wages of the bakers would be included in COGS.

Operating expenses are the costs required to run the day-to-day operations of the business. These can be further divided into selling, general, and administrative (SG&A) expenses. Selling expenses include costs directly related to the sale of goods or services, such as advertising, sales commissions, and shipping. General and administrative expenses encompass costs like salaries of administrative staff, office supplies, and utilities. For instance, the rent for a company's headquarters and the salaries of its HR team would fall under administrative expenses.

Non-operating expenses are costs not directly tied to the core business operations. These can include interest expenses on loans, loss on sale of assets, and other miscellaneous costs. While these expenses might not be central to the company's main activities, they can still significantly impact the overall profitability. For example, high-interest expenses due to substantial debt can erode the profits of a company despite strong operating performance.

The income statement often includes a section for gains and losses, which captures the financial impact of non-recurring events. Gains refer to profits from activities other than the company's primary operations, such as selling a piece of equipment for more than its book value. Losses, conversely, represent the financial impact of non-recurring negative events, such as damage from a natural disaster. These items are important to note because they can significantly affect the net income but do not reflect the ongoing operational performance.

Gross profit is a key figure derived from the income statement, calculated by subtracting COGS from total revenue. It indicates the efficiency of production and the company's ability to manage direct costs. For instance, if a company's gross profit is declining, it might indicate rising production costs or pricing pressures, necessitating a review of operations and cost management strategies.

Operating profit, also known as operating income, is determined by subtracting operating expenses from gross profit. This metric provides insight into the company's efficiency in managing its regular business activities. A high operating profit margin suggests that the company is effective in controlling its operating costs relative to its revenue. For example, a company with streamlined operations and efficient cost management will typically exhibit a strong operating profit margin.

Net income, also known as net profit or bottom line, is the ultimate measure of a company's profitability. It is calculated by subtracting all expenses, including COGS, operating expenses, and non-operating expenses, from total revenue. Net income is a critical indicator of the company's overall financial health and is closely monitored by investors and analysts. For example, consistent growth in net income over time is a positive sign of a company's financial stability and growth potential.

In addition to these core elements, the income statement may include sections for earnings before interest and taxes (EBIT) and earnings before interest, taxes, depreciation, and amortization (EBITDA). EBIT measures a company's profitability from its core operations, excluding interest and tax expenses, providing a clearer view of operational efficiency. EBITDA adds back depreciation and amortization, offering a perspective on the company's cash flow from operations. These metrics are particularly useful for comparing performance across companies and industries, as they exclude factors that can vary significantly between businesses.

Understanding the income statement also involves recognizing its limitations. While it provides valuable insights into profitability and performance, it does not capture the company's cash flow or financial position. Therefore, it is essential to analyze the income statement in conjunction with the balance sheet and cash flow statement for a comprehensive view of the company's financial health. For instance, a company might show strong net income but have poor cash flow due to delayed payments from customers or high capital expenditures.

Analyzing trends in the income statement over multiple periods is crucial for identifying patterns and making informed decisions. For example, a consistent increase in revenue and net income over several quarters can indicate robust business growth and effective management. Conversely, declining revenue or increasing expenses might signal potential issues that need to be addressed. Comparing the income statement with industry benchmarks can also provide valuable insights into the company's competitive position and operational efficiency.

Ratio analysis is another powerful tool for interpreting the income statement. Key ratios such as gross profit margin, operating profit margin, and net profit margin help assess profitability at different stages of the business process. Return on sales (ROS), calculated as net income divided by total revenue, measures the efficiency of converting sales into profits. For example, a high ROS indicates that the company is effective in controlling costs and maximizing profitability from its sales activities.

The income statement is also essential for forecasting and budgeting. By analyzing historical income statements, businesses can identify trends and patterns that inform future projections. This helps in setting realistic financial goals, allocating resources effectively, and planning for growth. For instance, if a company observes a seasonal increase in sales during certain periods, it can plan inventory and staffing accordingly to optimize performance.

In conclusion, the income statement is a vital financial document that provides a comprehensive overview of a company's revenues, expenses, and profitability. It offers valuable insights into the operational efficiency and financial health of the business, making it an essential tool for managers, investors, and stakeholders. By understanding the components of the income statement and employing various analytical techniques, beginners can gain a deeper understanding of a company's financial performance and make informed decisions. Regular analysis and comparison with industry benchmarks further enhance the utility of the income statement, helping businesses drive growth and achieve long-term success. Understanding the income statement also involves recognizing its limitations. While it provides valuable insights into profitability and performance, it does not capture the company's cash flow or financial position. Therefore, it is essential to analyze the income statement in conjunction with the balance sheet and cash flow statement for a comprehensive view of the company's financial health. For instance, a company might show strong net income but have poor cash flow due to delayed payments from customers or high capital expenditures.

Cash Flow Statement

The cash flow statement is an essential financial document that provides a detailed account of a company's cash inflows and outflows over a specific period. Unlike the income statement, which focuses on profitability, the cash flow statement reveals the liquidity and solvency of the business, highlighting its ability to generate cash to meet its obligations. Understanding the cash flow statement is crucial for beginners as it offers a clear picture of how cash is managed and utilized within the company.

The cash flow statement is divided into three main sections: operating activities, investing activities, and financing activities. Each section provides insights into different aspects of cash management and helps stakeholders understand the sources and uses of cash.

Operating activities are the core business operations that generate revenue and incur expenses. This section of the cash flow statement adjusts net income for changes in working capital and non-cash items like depreciation and amortization. For instance, if a company makes a sale and the customer pays immediately, the cash inflow from that sale is recorded in the operating activities. Conversely, if the customer buys on credit, the sale will appear as revenue on the income statement, but it will not generate immediate cash flow until the payment is received. This adjustment is vital because it reflects the true cash generated from regular business activities, excluding accounting adjustments.

The operating activities section also adjusts for changes in accounts receivable, accounts payable, inventory, and other working capital components. For example, an increase in accounts receivable indicates that more sales were made on credit, which reduces cash flow. Similarly, an increase in inventory represents money spent on purchasing goods that have not yet been sold, impacting cash availability. By examining these adjustments, stakeholders can assess how effectively a company is managing its day-to-day operations and working capital.

Investing activities encompass the purchase and sale of long-term assets and investments. This section includes transactions involving property, plant, equipment, and investments in other companies. For example, if a company buys new machinery, the cash outflow will be recorded under investing activities. Conversely, selling a piece of equipment or a business unit would generate a cash inflow in this section. Investing activities provide insights into a company's growth strategy and capital expenditures. A business that continually invests in new assets may be focusing on expansion and long-term growth, while significant asset sales might indicate a need to raise cash or streamline operations.

The financing activities section records cash flows related to borrowing, repaying debt, issuing stock, and paying dividends. This section reflects how a company finances its operations and growth through external sources. For example, if a company issues new shares, the cash inflow from this transaction is recorded under financing activities. Similarly, taking out a loan or repaying the principal amount of a loan would be included in this section. Paying dividends to shareholders also appears here as a cash outflow. Analyzing financing activities helps stakeholders understand the company's capital structure, debt levels, and policies regarding shareholder returns.

One critical aspect of the cash flow statement is its ability to highlight discrepancies between net income and actual cash flow. A company may report high net income on the income statement but still face cash flow problems if it has significant non-cash expenses or poor working capital management. For instance, a business might show substantial profits due to large sales on credit, but if customers delay payments, the company could struggle to meet its financial obligations. The cash flow statement bridges this gap by providing a clearer picture of the company's cash position.

A practical example of the importance of the cash flow statement can be seen in the case of a startup company. Startups often experience rapid growth and may report impressive revenue figures. However, they also tend to reinvest heavily in product development, marketing, and expansion. These investments, while essential for growth, can lead to negative cash flow from operations. By examining the cash flow statement, investors can determine whether the startup has sufficient cash reserves or access to financing to sustain its growth trajectory.

Another example is a mature company with stable revenues and profits. Such a company might generate consistent positive cash flow from operations. However, if it decides to undertake a major capital project, such as building a new factory, the investing activities section of the cash flow statement will show significant cash outflows. Stakeholders can then assess whether the company has adequate cash flow from operations or needs to raise additional funds through financing activities.

For beginners, it's important to understand that the cash flow statement provides a dynamic view of the company's financial health. Unlike the balance sheet, which is a snapshot at a specific point in time, and the income statement, which covers a period but focuses on profitability, the cash flow statement offers a real-time perspective on cash movements. This dynamic view is crucial for assessing a company's ability to generate cash, meet its obligations, and invest in future growth.

One practical tip for beginners is to pay close attention to the net cash provided by operating activities. A consistently positive figure indicates that the company is generating sufficient cash from its core operations to sustain itself. On the other hand, a consistently negative figure could signal cash flow problems, even if the company reports positive net income. Such a scenario might require deeper analysis to identify the root causes, such as poor working capital management, excessive credit sales, or high non-cash expenses.

Another useful tip is to compare the cash flow statement with the income statement and balance sheet. This comprehensive analysis helps identify any discrepancies and provides a holistic view of the company's financial health. For example, if a company shows strong net income but weak operating cash flow, it might be relying heavily on credit sales or facing issues with collecting receivables. Conversely, a company with modest net income but strong operating cash flow could be effectively managing its cash resources and operating efficiently.

Understanding the cash flow statement also involves recognizing the impact of different accounting methods. For example, the direct method of presenting operating cash flows lists specific cash inflows and outflows, providing a straightforward view of cash transactions. The indirect method, more commonly used, starts with net income and adjusts for non-cash items and changes in working capital. Both methods ultimately provide the same net cash flow from operating activities but offer different perspectives on cash flow components.

In conclusion, the cash flow statement is a vital financial document that offers insights into a company's liquidity, solvency, and overall financial health. By examining the cash flows from operating, investing, and financing activities, stakeholders can gain a comprehensive understanding of how cash is generated and utilized within the business. For beginners, mastering the cash flow statement is crucial for making informed decisions, assessing financial performance, and planning for future growth. Regular analysis and comparison with other financial statements enhance its utility, helping businesses navigate the complexities of cash management and achieve long-term success. Understanding the cash flow statement is essential not only for investors and financial analysts but also for business managers and owners. Effective cash flow management can mean the difference between success and failure, especially for small and medium-sized enterprises (SMEs). Here are some specific strategies and practices to optimize cash flow and ensure financial stability.

Statement of Retained Earnings

The statement of retained earnings is a crucial financial document that outlines changes in a company's retained earnings over a specific period. It bridges the gap between the income statement and the balance sheet, showing how profits are used— whether reinvested in the business or distributed as dividends to shareholders. Understanding this statement is essential for beginners, as it provides insights into a company's reinvestment strategies and financial health.

Retained earnings represent the cumulative amount of net income that a company retains rather than distributing to shareholders as dividends. These earnings are reinvested in the business to fund operations, expand capacity, or pay down debt. The statement of retained earnings starts with the beginning balance of retained earnings, adds net income for the period, subtracts any dividends paid, and adjusts for any other changes, such as prior period adjustments or corrections of errors.

Imagine a small business owner, Sarah, who runs a successful bakery. At the beginning of the year, her bakery's retained earnings were $50,000. During the year, the bakery earned a net income of $30,000 and paid $10,000 in dividends to its shareholders. The statement of retained earnings would show an increase in retained earnings of $20,000, resulting in an ending balance of $70,000. This simple example illustrates how retained earnings grow when net income is retained and shrink when dividends are paid out.

Net income is a key component of the statement of retained earnings. It is the profit a company makes after all expenses, taxes, and costs are subtracted from total revenue. For Sarah's bakery, the $30,000 net income reflects the profitability of her business operations for the year. This figure is directly transferred from the income statement to the statement of retained earnings.

Dividends are another critical factor. They represent the portion of net income distributed to shareholders. Dividends can be in the form of cash payments, additional shares of stock, or other assets. In our example, Sarah decided to pay $10,000 in cash dividends to her shareholders. This action reduces the retained earnings because it is a distribution of the profits rather than a reinvestment in the business.

Prior period adjustments may also affect the statement of retained earnings. These adjustments correct errors or account for changes in accounting principles from previous periods. For instance, if Sarah discovered that she had underreported expenses in the previous year, she would need to adjust the beginning retained earnings balance to reflect the corrected net income. This ensures that the retained earnings accurately represent the cumulative profits and losses of the business.

The statement of retained earnings is closely linked to the income statement and the balance sheet. It uses net income from the income statement and impacts the equity section of the balance sheet. By understanding these connections, beginners can gain a comprehensive view of how financial statements interact and reflect a company's financial position.

For instance, if Sarah's bakery consistently generates high net income but also pays out substantial dividends, the retained earnings may grow slowly.

Conversely, if the bakery retains most of its earnings, the retained earnings will accumulate more rapidly, providing a larger internal source of funding for growth and expansion.

Consider the case of a technology startup, TechVision, which has been in operation for five years. The company has experienced rapid growth and generated significant net income each year. However, rather than paying dividends, TechVision has chosen to retain all its earnings to reinvest in research and development, expand its product lines, and enter new markets. As a result, TechVision's retained earnings have grown substantially, providing a strong financial foundation for future growth and innovation.

In contrast, a mature company in a stable industry might adopt a different strategy. Take, for example, a utility company that has been operating for decades. This company generates steady, predictable income and has limited opportunities for significant expansion. Therefore, it might choose to distribute a larger portion of its net income as dividends to shareholders. This approach provides a regular income stream for investors while maintaining sufficient retained earnings to fund necessary maintenance and upgrades.

Retained earnings can also be affected by stock dividends and stock splits. Stock dividends involve issuing additional shares to shareholders, which transfers a portion of retained earnings to the common stock account. This action does not impact the total equity but reallocates it within the equity section. Stock splits, on the other hand, increase the number of shares outstanding and reduce the per-share value, but do not affect the total retained earnings or equity.

Understanding the statement of retained earnings also involves recognizing its role in assessing dividend policies. Companies with stable, growing retained earnings are often seen as financially healthy and capable of sustaining or increasing dividend payments. Investors and analysts use this information to evaluate a company's long-term viability and investment potential.

For beginners, it is essential to grasp the strategic implications of retained earnings. Companies must balance the benefits of reinvesting profits with the expectations of shareholders for dividend payments. A business that retains most of its earnings might be focusing on growth and expansion, while one that pays high dividends might be prioritizing shareholder returns.

Consider a family-owned manufacturing company that has been passed down through generations. The current owner, Maria, faces a decision: reinvest the substantial profits into modernizing the production facilities or distribute the profits as dividends to family members who are shareholders. By analyzing the statement of retained earnings, Maria can assess the long-term impact of each option. Reinvesting the profits could lead to increased efficiency and future growth, while paying dividends might satisfy immediate shareholder expectations.

The statement of retained earnings also provides insights into a company's financial strategy during economic downturns. During challenging times, companies might reduce or suspend dividend payments to preserve cash and strengthen their financial position. This approach can be seen during the 2008 financial crisis when many companies cut dividends to maintain liquidity and navigate the economic turbulence.

In conclusion, the statement of retained earnings is a vital financial document that offers a detailed view of how a company manages its profits. By understanding the components and implications of this statement, beginners can gain valuable insights into a company's financial health, strategic decisions, and long-term potential. Whether a business chooses to reinvest its earnings or distribute them as dividends, the statement of retained earnings provides a clear picture of its financial priorities and capabilities. Through careful analysis and strategic planning, effective management of retained earnings can support sustainable growth, shareholder satisfaction, and overall financial stability. Effective management of retained earnings requires a clear understanding of the company's goals, market conditions, and shareholder expectations. By aligning retained earnings strategies with these factors, businesses can optimize their financial performance and ensure long-term success.

How to Analyze Financial Statements

Analyzing financial statements is a fundamental skill for anyone looking to understand the financial health and performance of a business. These statements provide a structured way to assess a company's profitability, liquidity, and solvency, and they can guide decision-making processes for investors, managers, and other stakeholders.

To start, it's essential to understand the three primary financial statements: the income statement, the balance sheet, and the cash flow statement. Each offers distinct insights into different aspects of a company's financial situation.

The income statement, also known as the profit and loss statement, outlines the company's revenues, expenses, and profits over a specific period. It begins with the total revenue generated from sales and other income sources. From this, the cost of goods sold (COGS) is subtracted to find the gross profit. Operating expenses, such as salaries, rent, and utilities, are then deducted to determine the operating profit. Finally, after accounting for interest, taxes, and other non-operating items, the net income is calculated. This bottom-line figure indicates the company's profitability during the period.

Imagine a coffee shop owned by Emma. Her income statement for the year shows $200,000 in total revenue. The cost of goods sold, including coffee beans, milk, and pastries, amounts to $60,000. This leaves her with a gross profit of $140,000. After deducting $90,000 in operating expenses, including rent, salaries, and utilities, her operating profit is $50,000. After accounting for $5,000 in interest on a loan and $10,000 in taxes, her net income is $35,000. This net income figure provides a clear picture of Emma's coffee shop's profitability.

Next, the balance sheet provides a snapshot of a company's financial position at a specific point in time. It consists of three main sections: assets, liabilities, and shareholders' equity. Assets are what the company owns, including cash, inventory, and property. Liabilities are what the company owes, such as loans and accounts payable. Shareholders' equity represents the owners' claim on the assets after all liabilities have been paid off. The balance sheet follows the fundamental accounting equation: Assets = Liabilities + Shareholders' Equity.

Consider a small tech startup. Its balance sheet shows $500,000 in total assets, including $200,000 in cash, $100,000 in accounts receivable, and $200,000 in equipment. The company has $150,000 in liabilities, including a $100,000 loan and $50,000 in accounts payable. The shareholders' equity, therefore, is $350,000. This balance sheet reveals the company's financial stability and how it finances its operations, either through debt or equity.

The cash flow statement complements the income statement and the balance sheet by showing how cash moves in and out of the business. It is divided into three sections: cash flows from operating activities, investing activities, and financing activities. Operating activities include cash transactions related to the company's core business operations, such as receipts from sales and payments to suppliers. Investing activities cover cash spent on or received from the purchase and sale of assets like equipment or investments. Financing activities detail cash flows from borrowing and repaying loans or issuing and buying back stock.

For example, a manufacturing company's cash flow statement might show $100,000 in net cash from operating activities, indicating strong operational performance. It also shows a $50,000 outflow in investing activities due to the purchase of new machinery and a $20,000 inflow from financing activities due to a new loan. This statement helps stakeholders understand the company's liquidity and how it generates and uses cash.

Analyzing these financial statements involves several key techniques and ratios. One common approach is horizontal analysis, which compares financial data over multiple periods to identify trends and growth patterns. For instance, if Emma's coffee shop had a net income of $20,000 last year and $35,000 this year, horizontal analysis reveals a 75% increase in profitability. This trend indicates that her business is growing and becoming more profitable over time.

Vertical analysis, on the other hand, involves comparing each item on a financial statement to a base figure within the same period. In an income statement, this often means expressing each expense as a percentage of total revenue. For Emma's coffee shop, if her total revenue is $200,000 and rent is $30,000, rent accounts for 15% of her revenue. This analysis helps identify the proportion of revenue consumed by various expenses, allowing Emma to control costs more effectively.

Ratio analysis is another powerful tool. It involves calculating and interpreting various financial ratios to assess a company's performance and financial health. Key ratios include:

- **Liquidity Ratios:** These measure a company's ability to meet short-term obligations. The current ratio, calculated as current assets divided by current liabilities, indicates whether the company has enough assets to cover its short-term debts. A current ratio above 1 generally suggests good liquidity.

- **Profitability Ratios:** These assess a company's ability to generate profit relative to sales, assets, or equity. The net profit margin, calculated as net income divided by total revenue, shows how much profit is generated from each dollar of sales. A higher net profit margin indicates better profitability.

- **Solvency Ratios:** These measure a company's ability to meet long-term obligations. The debt-to-equity ratio, calculated as total liabilities divided by shareholders' equity, indicates the relative proportion of debt and equity financing. A lower ratio suggests a more financially stable company with less reliance on debt.

- **Efficiency Ratios:** These assess how effectively a company uses its assets. The inventory turnover ratio, calculated as the cost of goods sold divided by average inventory, shows how quickly inventory is sold and replaced. A higher ratio indicates efficient inventory management.

Consider a retail business with a current ratio of 2, a net profit margin of 10%, a debt-to-equity ratio of 0.5, and an inventory turnover ratio of 8. These ratios suggest the business has strong liquidity, good profitability, low financial risk, and efficient inventory management.

In addition to these techniques, it's important to consider qualitative factors when analyzing financial statements. These include the company's competitive position, management quality, industry conditions, and economic environment. For instance, a company operating in a rapidly growing industry might show robust financial performance, but understanding the competitive dynamics and potential risks is crucial for a comprehensive analysis.

Furthermore, benchmarking against industry peers can provide valuable context. Comparing a company's financial ratios with those of similar businesses helps identify strengths and weaknesses. For example, if Emma's coffee shop has a net profit margin of 18% while the industry average is 12%, it indicates that her business is more profitable than its peers.

Analyzing financial statements also involves looking for red flags that might indicate financial distress or accounting irregularities. These could include declining revenues, increasing debt levels, unusual changes in financial ratios, or discrepancies between cash flow and net income. Identifying such warning signs early can help stakeholders take corrective actions to mitigate risks.

In conclusion, analyzing financial statements is a multifaceted process that requires a combination of quantitative techniques and qualitative judgment. By thoroughly understanding and interpreting the income statement, balance sheet, and cash flow statement, beginners can gain valuable insights into a company's financial health and performance. This knowledge not only aids in making informed investment and management decisions but also enhances one's ability to navigate the complex world of business finance effectively. A critical aspect of financial statement analysis is understanding the broader context within which a company operates. This includes macroeconomic factors, industry trends, and competitive pressures. For instance, a company might show strong financial results, but if it operates in an industry facing significant headwinds, such as regulatory changes or technological disruptions, these external factors must be considered.

Chapter 4

Cash Flow Management

Importance of Cash Flow

Cash flow is the lifeblood of any business. It represents the movement of money in and out of a company, and understanding its dynamics is crucial for maintaining the health and sustainability of an enterprise. Without sufficient cash flow, even profitable businesses can falter. Therefore, grasping the importance of cash flow is essential for entrepreneurs, managers, and investors alike.

Consider a small bakery run by John. He bakes the most delicious pastries in town, and his sales are booming. However, John faces a constant struggle to pay his suppliers and employees on time. Despite strong sales, his business suffers from cash flow problems because his customers pay him on credit, taking up to 60 days to settle their invoices. This delay creates a gap between when he incurs expenses and when he receives payment, highlighting the critical need for effective cash flow management.

Cash flow can be broadly categorized into three types: operating, investing, and financing cash flows. Operating cash flow refers to the cash generated or consumed by a company's core business operations. It includes receipts from sales of goods and services and payments for expenses such as salaries, rent, and utilities. Positive operating cash flow indicates that a business's core activities are generating enough cash to sustain its operations, which is a strong indicator of financial health.

Investing cash flow relates to cash used for or generated from investments in assets such as property, equipment, or securities. For example, if John decides to buy a new oven for his bakery, the cash spent on this purchase would be recorded as an outflow in the investing section of his cash flow statement. Conversely, if he sells an old piece of equipment, the proceeds would be an inflow. Investing activities typically reflect a company's growth strategy and capital expenditure plans.

Financing cash flow consists of cash transactions related to raising or repaying capital, such as issuing shares, taking out loans, or repaying debt. If John takes out a loan to expand his bakery, the loan amount will be a financing cash inflow, while the repayments will be outflows. This section of the cash flow statement shows how a company funds its operations and growth through external sources of capital.

One of the key reasons cash flow is so important is that it ensures a business can meet its short-term obligations. Regular and sufficient cash inflows allow a company to pay its bills, salaries, and other operating expenses without delay. For John, managing cash flow effectively means he can pay his suppliers on time, which helps maintain good relationships and ensures a steady supply of ingredients for his bakery.

Moreover, positive cash flow provides a buffer against unexpected expenses or economic downturns.

Businesses with strong cash reserves are better positioned to weather periods of reduced revenue or increased costs. For instance, if John's bakery experiences a sudden drop in sales due to a local event or economic slowdown, having a healthy cash flow can help him navigate this challenging period without resorting to emergency loans or drastic cost-cutting measures.

Cash flow is also a critical factor in determining a company's ability to invest in growth opportunities. A business with ample cash flow can take advantage of favorable market conditions, invest in new projects, or expand its operations. For example, if John's bakery consistently generates positive cash flow, he might consider opening a second location or launching a new product line. These growth initiatives can drive future revenue and profitability, but they require upfront investment, which is only feasible with solid cash flow management.

Investors and lenders closely scrutinize a company's cash flow statements when making investment or lending decisions. Positive and consistent cash flow is often seen as a sign of a financially stable and well-managed business. Conversely, negative cash flow or erratic cash flow patterns can raise red flags, prompting further investigation or leading to funding rejections. For John, demonstrating strong cash flow can help attract investors or secure favorable loan terms, providing the financial support needed for expansion.

Furthermore, cash flow analysis can offer insights into a company's operational efficiency and financial practices. By examining the cash flow statement, stakeholders can identify trends, inefficiencies, or areas for improvement. For instance, if John notices that a significant portion of his cash is tied up in accounts receivable, he might implement stricter credit policies or offer discounts for early payments to improve cash inflows. Similarly, if a large amount of cash is consistently used for inventory purchases, he might explore better inventory management techniques to reduce holding costs and free up cash.

Effective cash flow management also involves forecasting future cash flows to anticipate potential shortfalls or surpluses. By projecting cash inflows and outflows based on historical data and future plans, businesses can make informed decisions and take proactive measures. For John, creating a cash flow forecast can help him plan for seasonal fluctuations in sales, ensuring he has enough cash to cover expenses during slower periods and can build up reserves during peak seasons.

In addition to internal management, cash flow plays a crucial role in strategic planning and decision-making. Business leaders use cash flow analysis to evaluate the feasibility and impact of major decisions such as mergers, acquisitions, or capital projects. For example, if John is considering acquiring a competitor's bakery, a thorough cash flow analysis can help him assess whether the acquisition is financially viable and how it will affect his overall cash position.

Another aspect of cash flow importance lies in its impact on shareholder value. Companies that generate strong and consistent cash flow are often able to return value to shareholders through dividends or share buybacks. For publicly traded companies, this can enhance investor confidence and support stock price appreciation. While John's bakery might be privately owned, the principle remains the same: strong cash flow can enable owners to reinvest in the business or distribute profits, creating value for stakeholders.

It's also worth noting that cash flow problems can sometimes be indicative of deeper issues within the business. Persistent negative cash flow may signal underlying problems such as declining sales, poor cost management, or inefficiencies in operations. For John, recognizing and addressing cash flow issues early can prevent more severe financial difficulties and help steer his bakery back on track.

In summary, the importance of cash flow cannot be overstated. It is essential for meeting short-term obligations, providing a buffer against uncertainties, enabling growth investments, attracting investors and lenders, and supporting strategic decision-making. For John and other business owners, effective cash flow management is a cornerstone of financial health and stability. By understanding and actively managing cash flow, businesses can navigate challenges, seize opportunities, and build a foundation for long-term success. Additionally, cash flow management is integral to maintaining operational flexibility. When a company has a strong cash flow position, it can respond more quickly to market opportunities or challenges. For example, John's bakery might suddenly see a surge in demand for a new type of pastry. With adequate cash flow, he can swiftly purchase additional supplies, hire temporary staff, or invest in marketing to capitalize on this trend.

Conversely, if cash flow is tight, he might miss out on these opportunities due to a lack of available funds.

Techniques for Improving Cash Flow

Effective cash flow management is crucial for the sustainability and growth of any business. By implementing various techniques to improve cash flow, businesses can ensure they meet their financial obligations, invest in growth opportunities, and safeguard against economic uncertainties. For entrepreneurs and managers, understanding and applying these techniques can make the difference between merely surviving and truly thriving in the marketplace.

One of the most straightforward techniques to improve cash flow is to accelerate the inflow of cash. This can be achieved by optimizing the billing and collections process. Businesses should invoice their customers immediately upon delivery of goods or services. Delays in invoicing can result in delayed payments, which in turn can strain cash flow. To further expedite collections, offering discounts for early payments can be an effective strategy. For instance, a 2% discount for payments made within 10 days can incentivize customers to pay sooner, thus improving cash inflows.

On the flip side, extending payment terms with suppliers can help businesses retain cash for a longer period. Negotiating longer payment terms, such as 60 or 90 days instead of the standard 30 days, can provide a buffer, allowing businesses to use the cash for other immediate needs. However, it's essential to maintain a good relationship with suppliers. Open communication and transparent negotiations can lead to mutually beneficial agreements without jeopardizing supplier relationships.

Inventory management also plays a significant role in cash flow improvement. Holding excessive inventory ties up cash that could otherwise be used for other operational needs. Implementing just-in-time (JIT) inventory systems can help reduce the amount of cash tied up in stock. By ordering inventory only as needed, businesses can minimize holding costs and free up cash. However, this approach requires precise demand forecasting and reliable suppliers to avoid stockouts and disruptions.

Another effective technique is to lease rather than purchase equipment. Leasing can significantly reduce the upfront cash outflow compared to purchasing. While leasing may result in higher long-term costs, the immediate benefit is improved cash flow. For example, a construction company might lease heavy machinery instead of buying it outright, thus preserving cash for other operational expenses or unexpected needs.

Businesses can also improve cash flow by optimizing pricing strategies. Regularly reviewing and adjusting pricing can ensure that products or services are sold at a rate that covers costs and generates a healthy margin. It's important to consider market conditions, competitor pricing, and the perceived value of the offering. Raising prices, even by a small percentage, can have a significant positive impact on cash flow if done strategically and communicated effectively to customers.

Cost control is another critical aspect of cash flow management. Conducting regular reviews of all expenses can identify areas where costs can be trimmed without compromising quality or operational efficiency. For instance, renegotiating contracts with service providers, switching to more cost-effective suppliers, or reducing discretionary spending can result in significant savings. Implementing energy-saving measures or adopting technology that improves operational efficiency can also reduce ongoing costs.

Diversifying revenue streams can also enhance cash flow. Relying on a single source of income can be risky, especially if that source is subject to seasonal fluctuations or market volatility. By diversifying, businesses can create a more stable and predictable cash flow. For instance, a retail store that traditionally relies on in-store sales might develop an online presence to reach a broader customer base and generate additional revenue.

In some cases, businesses might consider factoring their receivables to improve cash flow. Factoring involves selling accounts receivable to a third party at a discount in exchange for immediate cash. While this approach provides quick access to cash, it comes at a cost, as the factor will take a percentage of the receivables as a fee. This technique can be particularly useful for businesses that experience long payment cycles or need immediate cash to cover operational expenses.

Implementing robust cash flow forecasting is essential for anticipating future cash needs and avoiding potential shortfalls. By regularly projecting cash inflows and outflows, businesses can identify periods of cash surplus or deficit and take proactive measures. For example, a seasonal business that experiences fluctuations in revenue throughout the year can use cash flow forecasting to plan for lean periods, ensuring they have sufficient cash reserves to cover expenses during slow months.

Encouraging customers to pay via direct debit can also streamline cash inflows and reduce the risk of late payments. Direct debit arrangements ensure that payments are automatically deducted from customers' bank accounts on agreed dates, providing a steady and predictable cash flow. This method is particularly effective for businesses with recurring billing cycles, such as subscription services or utility providers.

For businesses with significant debt, refinancing existing loans can improve cash flow by reducing monthly debt service obligations. By negotiating lower interest rates or extending loan terms, businesses can lower their monthly payments, freeing up cash for other uses. However, it's important to carefully consider the long-term implications of refinancing, as extending loan terms can result in higher overall interest costs.

Improving cash flow also involves managing receivables diligently. Establishing clear credit policies and conducting thorough credit checks before extending credit to customers can minimize the risk of bad debts. Additionally, implementing a systematic follow-up process for overdue invoices can ensure timely collections. This might involve sending regular reminders, making follow-up calls, or even engaging a collections agency if necessary.

Automating financial processes can provide significant benefits in cash flow management. Utilizing accounting software that integrates with invoicing, inventory, and payment systems can streamline operations, reduce errors, and provide real-time insights into cash flow status. Automation can also facilitate more accurate cash flow forecasting and help businesses respond more quickly to financial trends and issues.

Finally, maintaining a cash reserve or emergency fund is a prudent practice for managing cash flow. Setting aside a portion of cash inflows into a reserve fund can provide a financial cushion during unexpected downturns or emergencies. This practice ensures that businesses have a safety net to cover short-term cash flow gaps without resorting to high-interest loans or other costly financing options.

In conclusion, improving cash flow requires a multifaceted approach that encompasses accelerating cash inflows, managing outflows, optimizing pricing, controlling costs, diversifying revenue streams, and leveraging financial tools and strategies. By diligently applying these techniques, businesses can enhance their financial health, ensuring they have the liquidity needed to operate smoothly, seize opportunities, and navigate challenges. For entrepreneurs and managers, mastering these techniques is essential for building a resilient and successful business. Building strong relationships with stakeholders is another way to improve cash flow. Open and transparent communication with customers, suppliers, and creditors can lead to more favorable payment terms and conditions. For example, long-term partnerships with suppliers might enable businesses to negotiate bulk purchase discounts or extended credit terms, which can significantly enhance cash flow. Similarly, cultivating good relationships with customers can lead to timely payments and repeat business, both of which are beneficial for cash flow.

Cash Flow Forecasting

Cash flow forecasting is an essential practice for any business, providing a clear picture of future financial health and enabling proactive management of funds. Accurate forecasting helps businesses anticipate cash shortages, avoid crises, and make informed decisions about investments and expenditures. Mastering this skill can significantly enhance a company's ability to navigate financial challenges and capitalize on growth opportunities.

To begin with, understanding the foundation of cash flow forecasting is crucial. Cash flow forecasting involves projecting the expected cash inflows and outflows over a specific period, typically monthly, quarterly, or annually. This projection includes all sources of income, such as sales revenue, loans, and investments, as well as all expenditures, including operating costs, loan repayments, and capital investments. By comparing projected cash inflows with outflows, businesses can identify periods of cash surplus or deficit and plan accordingly.

One effective approach to cash flow forecasting is the direct method, which focuses on actual cash transactions. This method involves listing all expected cash receipts and payments to calculate the net cash flow. For example, a retail business might project cash inflows from sales, credit card payments, and loans, while considering outflows for inventory purchases, rent, utilities, and payroll. This method provides a detailed and realistic view of the company's cash position.

Alternatively, the indirect method starts with net income and adjusts for non-cash items and changes in working capital. This approach is often used for long-term forecasting and provides insights into how operational decisions impact cash flow. For instance, a manufacturer might begin with net income and adjust for depreciation, changes in inventory levels, and accounts receivable/payable to forecast cash flow. The indirect method helps in understanding the impact of profit on cash flow and identifying areas for improvement.

Regardless of the method used, accuracy in cash flow forecasting hinges on reliable data. Historical financial data provides a solid foundation for projections, as past trends often indicate future patterns. However, it's essential to adjust historical data for any anticipated changes, such as new product launches, market expansion, or economic conditions. For example, a software company launching a new product line should adjust its sales projections to reflect expected growth and marketing expenses.

Regularly updating forecasts is another critical aspect of effective cash flow management. Business environments are dynamic, and factors such as market conditions, customer behavior, and economic fluctuations can change rapidly. By reviewing and updating cash flow forecasts regularly, businesses can adapt to changes and make informed decisions. For instance, a restaurant might update its forecast monthly to account for seasonal variations in customer traffic and inventory costs.

Involving key stakeholders in the forecasting process enhances accuracy and accountability. Collaborating with department heads, financial advisors, and managers ensures that all aspects of the business are considered, and assumptions are realistic. For example, the sales team can provide insights into expected revenue, while the purchasing department can forecast inventory costs. This collaborative approach ensures that forecasts are comprehensive and grounded in practical knowledge.

Scenario analysis is a valuable technique for cash flow forecasting, allowing businesses to prepare for various outcomes. By creating multiple scenarios—such as best-case, worst-case, and most-likely—businesses can understand the potential impact of different variables on their cash flow. For instance, a construction company might develop scenarios based on different project timelines, cost overruns, and payment delays. This analysis helps in identifying risks and developing contingency plans.

Technology plays a significant role in enhancing cash flow forecasting. Advanced accounting software and financial tools can automate data collection, analysis, and reporting, reducing errors and saving time. These tools often come with built-in forecasting models and analytics, providing businesses with real-time insights into their cash flow. For instance, a retail chain might use software to integrate sales data, inventory levels, and expenses, generating accurate and timely cash flow forecasts.

Understanding the timing of cash flows is crucial for accurate forecasting. Not all cash inflows and outflows occur evenly throughout the month or year. For example, a business might receive most of its revenue at the beginning of the month but incur significant expenses mid-month. By mapping out the timing of cash transactions, businesses can identify potential shortfalls and take corrective actions, such as securing short-term financing or adjusting payment schedules.

Managing accounts receivable and payable effectively can significantly impact cash flow forecasting. Promptly invoicing customers and following up on overdue payments ensures steady cash inflows. On the other hand, negotiating favorable payment terms with suppliers can help delay cash outflows. For example, a wholesale distributor might offer discounts for early payments to customers while negotiating 60-day payment terms with suppliers. This balance helps in maintaining a positive cash flow.

Cash flow forecasting should also consider external factors that could impact the business. Economic conditions, industry trends, and regulatory changes can influence cash flows. For instance, a manufacturing company should monitor raw material prices and adjust forecasts based on market trends. Similarly, changes in tax laws or trade policies can affect cash inflows and outflows, requiring adjustments to forecasts.

Communicating cash flow forecasts effectively within the organization is essential for alignment and decision-making. Clear and concise reports that highlight key insights and risks help stakeholders understand the business's financial position. Regular meetings to discuss forecasts and financial performance ensure that everyone is on the same page and can contribute to achieving cash flow targets. For example, a weekly finance meeting might review the latest forecast, discuss variances, and plan actions to address any issues.

Maintaining a cash reserve or buffer is a prudent practice for managing cash flow uncertainties. Setting aside a portion of cash inflows into a reserve fund provides a cushion during unexpected downturns or emergencies. This practice ensures that businesses have the liquidity needed to cover short-term cash flow gaps without resorting to high-interest loans or other costly financing options. For instance, a small business might maintain a cash reserve equivalent to three months' operating expenses to ensure stability.

Continuous improvement in cash flow forecasting processes can lead to better accuracy and reliability over time. Regularly reviewing forecasting accuracy and identifying areas for improvement helps businesses refine their models and assumptions. Seeking feedback from stakeholders and incorporating lessons learned from past forecasts contribute to a more robust forecasting process. For example, an annual review of forecasting performance might reveal that certain revenue streams were consistently overestimated, prompting adjustments for greater accuracy.

In conclusion, cash flow forecasting is a vital practice for ensuring the financial health and stability of a business. By understanding the fundamentals, leveraging technology, involving stakeholders, and continuously improving processes, businesses can achieve accurate and reliable cash flow forecasts. This proactive approach enables businesses to anticipate challenges, make informed decisions, and capitalize on opportunities, ultimately contributing to long-term success and growth. For entrepreneurs and managers, mastering cash flow forecasting is an essential skill that underpins effective financial management and strategic planning. Effective cash flow forecasting also involves a deep understanding of the business cycle and the external environment in which a company operates. For example, businesses in sectors like retail or tourism experience significant seasonal variations that must be factored into their forecasts. A retailer should anticipate higher cash inflows during the holiday season and plan for increased inventory purchases accordingly. Conversely, they should prepare for lower sales periods by managing expenses and preserving cash reserves.

Managing Receivables and Payables

Managing receivables and payables effectively is crucial for maintaining healthy cash flow and ensuring the financial stability of a business. These two aspects of working capital management directly impact liquidity, profitability, and overall business operations. Properly managing receivables and payables involves timely collection of outstanding invoices, strategic negotiation of payment terms, and diligent monitoring of both accounts.

Receivables, or accounts receivable, represent the money owed to a business by its customers for goods or services delivered but not yet paid for. Efficient management of receivables starts with establishing clear credit policies. These policies should define the terms under which customers can purchase on credit, including credit limits, payment terms, and the criteria used to assess creditworthiness. For instance, a company might offer net 30 terms, meaning payment is due 30 days from the invoice date, but only to customers with a strong credit history.

Once credit policies are in place, timely and accurate invoicing is essential. Delays in issuing invoices can lead to delays in payment, disrupting cash flow. Businesses should aim to send invoices as soon as goods are delivered or services rendered. Utilizing invoicing software can streamline this process, ensuring that invoices are sent promptly and reducing the likelihood of errors. For example, an e-commerce company might use automated invoicing to immediately bill customers upon purchase completion.

Monitoring receivables closely is another key practice. Regularly reviewing accounts receivable aging reports helps businesses identify overdue invoices and take appropriate action. These reports categorize outstanding invoices based on how long they have been unpaid, typically in 30-day increments. By identifying overdue accounts early, businesses can follow up with customers through reminders or calls, encouraging prompt payment. For instance, a wholesaler might notice several invoices overdue by 60 days and initiate contact with those customers to expedite payment.

Implementing an efficient collections process is vital for managing receivables. This process should include a series of steps for following up on overdue accounts, such as sending reminder emails, making phone calls, and, if necessary, engaging collection agencies. Maintaining a polite but firm approach in communications can help preserve customer relationships while ensuring payment. For example, a service provider might send a friendly reminder email one week after the due date, followed by a phone call if payment is not received within another week.

Offering incentives for early payment can also improve receivables management. Discounts for early payment, such as 2% off if paid within 10 days, can encourage customers to settle their accounts sooner, improving cash flow. While this reduces the amount collected slightly, the benefit of improved liquidity often outweighs the cost. For instance, a manufacturing company might offer a small discount to customers who pay their invoices within 10 days instead of the standard 30 days.

On the other side of the equation, managing payables, or accounts payable, involves handling the business's obligations to its suppliers and creditors. Effective payables management ensures that a business meets its obligations on time while optimizing cash flow. It starts with negotiating favorable payment terms with suppliers. By securing extended payment terms, businesses can hold onto their cash longer, improving liquidity. For example, negotiating 60-day terms instead of 30-day terms with suppliers can provide additional time to generate revenue from the goods purchased.

Prioritizing payments based on due dates and cash flow availability is crucial. Businesses should schedule payments to take advantage of the full credit period offered by suppliers without incurring late fees. Creating a payables calendar can help track upcoming payments and ensure that funds are available when needed. For instance, a retailer might schedule supplier payments strategically to coincide with periods of higher sales revenue.

Maintaining good relationships with suppliers is also important for managing payables effectively. Reliable suppliers are essential for smooth operations, and building strong relationships can lead to more favorable payment terms and greater flexibility. Regular communication, timely payments, and addressing any issues promptly can foster goodwill. For example, if a business occasionally needs to delay a payment, a strong relationship with the supplier might lead to more lenient payment terms during that period.

Monitoring accounts payable aging reports is as important as tracking receivables. These reports help businesses keep track of outstanding payables and prioritize payments based on due dates. By regularly reviewing aging reports, businesses can avoid late payments and maintain good credit standing. For instance, a construction company might use aging reports to ensure that subcontractors and material suppliers are paid on time, preventing project delays.

Balancing early payments with cash flow needs can be a strategic decision. While taking full advantage of credit terms is beneficial, some suppliers might offer discounts for early payment. Evaluating the cost-benefit of these discounts compared to the benefit of holding onto cash longer can help make informed decisions. For example, if a supplier offers a 2% discount for payment within 10 days, the business should consider whether the discount outweighs the benefit of using that cash for other purposes during the remaining credit period.

Integrating technology into the management of receivables and payables can streamline processes and improve accuracy. Accounting software and enterprise resource planning (ERP) systems can automate invoicing, payment scheduling, and reporting. These tools provide real-time visibility into cash flow and help identify potential issues before they become critical. For example, an ERP system can automatically generate aging reports, send payment reminders, and schedule payments, reducing manual effort and errors.

Regularly reconciling accounts is essential to ensure accuracy in receivables and payables. Reconciliation involves comparing internal records with external statements, such as bank statements and supplier invoices, to identify and resolve discrepancies. Timely reconciliation helps maintain accurate financial records and prevents issues such as duplicate payments or missed collections. For instance, a business might reconcile its accounts payable ledger with supplier statements monthly to ensure all payments are accounted for correctly.

Managing foreign currency transactions adds another layer of complexity to receivables and payables. Businesses operating internationally must consider exchange rate fluctuations and their impact on cash flow. Hedging strategies, such as forward contracts or options, can help mitigate currency risk and stabilize cash flows. For example, an exporter might use forward contracts to lock in exchange rates for future receivables, ensuring predictable cash inflows despite currency fluctuations.

Internal controls play a vital role in managing receivables and payables. Implementing robust controls helps prevent fraud, errors, and inefficiencies. Segregation of duties, authorization protocols, and regular audits are essential components of an effective control system. For example, ensuring that different employees handle invoicing, payment processing, and reconciliation reduces the risk of fraud and errors.

Training and development for staff involved in receivables and payables management can enhance efficiency and accuracy. Providing training on best practices, software tools, and internal processes ensures that employees are well-equipped to handle their responsibilities. Continuous professional development helps staff stay updated on industry trends and regulatory changes. For instance, a company might offer regular workshops on new accounting software features or changes in tax regulations.

Effective communication within the organization is crucial for managing receivables and payables. Ensuring that sales, finance, and procurement teams are aligned and share relevant information helps prevent issues such as overcommitting credit to customers or missing supplier payment deadlines. Regular meetings and clear communication channels facilitate collaboration and coordination. For example, a monthly meeting between the sales and finance teams can help align credit policies with sales goals and ensure timely invoicing and collections.

Ultimately, managing receivables and payables efficiently requires a proactive and strategic approach. By establishing clear policies, utilizing technology, maintaining strong relationships, and continuously monitoring and improving processes, businesses can optimize their cash flow, enhance financial stability, and support sustainable growth. The ability to manage receivables and payables effectively is a critical component of overall financial management and contributes significantly to a business's success. Ensuring that receivables and payables are handled with diligence not only impacts the immediate financial health of a business but also its long-term viability. For instance, consistent and efficient management of receivables enhances customer satisfaction and loyalty, as clients appreciate clear and fair credit terms along with timely and accurate invoicing. This, in turn, can lead to repeat business and positive word-of-mouth, contributing to sustained revenue growth.

Dealing with Cash Flow Problems

Cash flow problems can afflict businesses of all sizes, from fledgling startups to established enterprises. It's a situation where the outflow of cash exceeds the inflow, leading to a shortage that can hinder operations, delay growth, and, in severe cases, threaten the viability of the business. Understanding and managing cash flow effectively is essential to navigate these challenges and ensure the financial health of the organization.

One of the primary causes of cash flow problems is the mismatch between the timing of cash inflows and outflows. Businesses often face delays in receiving payments from customers, while their own obligations, such as payroll, rent, and supplier payments, are due on fixed dates. This discrepancy can create periods where cash on hand is insufficient to cover immediate needs. To address this, it's crucial to develop strategies that accelerate receivables and manage payables more effectively.

First and foremost, improving the speed of collections can significantly alleviate cash flow pressures. Implementing clear credit policies is the foundation. Define stringent credit terms and ensure they are communicated clearly to customers. For example, offering discounts for early payments can be an effective incentive. A common practice is to offer a small percentage discount if the invoice is paid within a certain period, say 2% off if paid within 10 days. This not only encourages prompt payment but also improves liquidity.

Automating the invoicing process is another critical step. Manual invoicing can lead to delays and errors, which in turn delay payments. By using invoicing software, businesses can ensure that invoices are issued promptly and accurately. Automated reminders can also be set up to follow up with customers who are approaching their due dates. This proactive approach helps in keeping the receivables cycle short and efficient.

Another strategy is to diversify payment options. Offering multiple ways for customers to pay, such as credit cards, electronic transfers, and online payment gateways, can expedite the payment process. The easier it is for customers to pay, the more likely they are to do so promptly. Additionally, establishing a clear collections procedure for overdue accounts is essential. This might involve a series of follow-up emails, phone calls, and possibly involving a collections agency if necessary. Maintaining a professional but firm approach is key to ensuring that overdue payments are collected without damaging customer relationships.

On the payables side, negotiating better terms with suppliers can provide much-needed breathing room. Extending payment terms, even by a few days, can make a significant difference. For instance, negotiating net 60 terms instead of net 30 can align payables more closely with receivables, reducing the gap. Building strong relationships with suppliers is advantageous in this aspect. Suppliers who trust in a business's reliability are more likely to extend favorable terms.

In addition to negotiating terms, managing the timing of payments strategically can improve cash flow. Prioritize payments based on due dates and cash availability, and consider taking full advantage of the credit period offered. However, be cautious not to delay payments excessively, as this can damage supplier relationships and potentially lead to supply disruptions.

Inventory management also plays a crucial role in cash flow management. Excess inventory ties up cash that could be used elsewhere in the business. Implementing an efficient inventory management system can help maintain optimal inventory levels. Techniques such as Just-In-Time (JIT) inventory can reduce the amount of cash tied up in stock by synchronizing inventory orders with production schedules and demand forecasts. Regularly reviewing inventory levels and sales data allows for adjustments that keep inventory lean and reduce carrying costs.

Expense management is another area where improvements can be made to ease cash flow problems. Conducting a thorough review of all business expenses can identify areas where costs can be cut or deferred. This might involve renegotiating contracts with service providers, finding more cost-effective alternatives, or eliminating non-essential expenditures. Even small savings can accumulate to make a significant impact on cash flow.

Forecasting and planning are indispensable tools in managing cash flow. Developing a detailed cash flow forecast helps in anticipating periods of cash shortages and surpluses. This forecast should account for all expected cash inflows and outflows, including sales, expenses, loan repayments, and capital expenditures. Regularly updating this forecast allows for adjustments to be made proactively, rather than reacting to cash flow crises as they occur.

In addition to forecasting, setting aside a cash reserve can provide a buffer during lean periods. This reserve acts as a safety net, ensuring that the business can continue to meet its obligations even when cash flow is tight. The size of the reserve will depend on the specific needs and risk profile of the business, but it's generally advisable to have enough to cover at least a few months of operating expenses.

Accessing external financing is another option to consider when dealing with cash flow problems. Lines of credit, short-term loans, and invoice financing can provide immediate cash to bridge gaps. For example, invoice financing allows businesses to receive an advance on outstanding invoices, providing liquidity without waiting for customers to pay. However, it's important to be mindful of the costs associated with these financing options and to use them judiciously.

Maintaining strong relationships with financial institutions can also be beneficial. Banks and lenders who are familiar with the business and have confidence in its management are more likely to provide favorable terms and support during difficult times. Regularly communicating with financial partners and keeping them informed about the business's performance and plans can help in securing necessary funding when needed.

www.ingramcontent.com/pod-product-compliance
Lightning Source LLC
Chambersburg PA
CBHW061322120726
48001CB00002B/645